SO-AEH-786

Praise for *The Metail Economy*

Evolving consumer needs are creating a new set of rules for companies. *The Metail Economy* does a brilliant job of highlighting what consumers expect, using powerful case studies of companies that have successfully addressed the heightened needs and wants of the most empowered generation of consumers yet. Joel Bines gives companies, big and small, key tools to succeed in this new environment.

> —**Hubert Joly**, senior lecturer at Harvard Business School, former Chairman and CEO of Best Buy, and author of *The Heart of Business: Leadership Principles for the Next Era of Capitalism*

As an expert in leadership, CEO succession, and executive success, I recognize how important it is for a leader to be able to look beyond the horizon. In this book, Joel Bines provides a map to do just that, identifying a critical and largely overlooked change in the relationship between consumers and the companies that hope to serve them, explaining the change in a direct and digestible way and providing a set of ideas to help adapt legacy thinking. This book is essential reading for any executive who aspires to the C-suite and hopes to remain relevant to today's demanding consumer.

> —**James M. Citrin**, leader of Spencer Stuart's North American CEO Practice and author of *Leading at a Distance: Practical Lessons for Virtual Success*

As an executive and board member, I have benefited from Joel's direct and to-the-point personality. His "voice" comes through loud and clear in this book. A must-read for every executive to understand the implications of what customer-centric truly means. Joel leverages his no-nonsense style to help make clear what companies must do to change their strategies before it is too late. A great action-oriented read!

—**Karen Katz**, former CEO of Neiman Marcus Group

What Bines identifies in *The Metail Economy* transcends commerce. The Me-centric mindset spills over into every aspect of business, from hiring and retaining talent to establishing authentic connections with all stakeholders.

—**Gena Smith**, SVP, HR and Head of Executive
    and Creative Recruitment at LVMH

As consumers, we each experience the shift in consumer power at retail, and Joel outlines clearly what companies *must* do to get ahead of the curve . . . not an option anymore.

—**Sergio Zyman**, bestselling author and former
    Chief Marketing Officer of Coca-Cola Company

The power inversion Bines identifies is real. Companies that do not understand the lessons in *The Metail Economy* risk falling short with their customers and behind their competition.

—**Michael Nicholson**, President and COO of J.Crew Group

The consumer revolution is upon us. *The Metail Economy*'s prescription is just what the doctor ordered.

—**Wanda Gierhart**, Global Chief Marketing and
    Content Officer of Cinemark

Too often, men and women in business forget they are consumers. This leads them to speak about customers—and employees—as "they" and "them," not as real people. By reminding us that we are all "Mes"—and that "Mes" are a constantly moving target that can't be taken for granted, even for a moment—Joel Bines has fired a warning shot over the bow of complacent companies and executives as well as providing a blueprint for success today and tomorrow.

—**Ryan Mathews**, globally renowned futurist and storyteller, bestselling author, and CEO of Black Monk Consulting

The Metail Economy identifies an important paradigm shift affecting all companies that hope to develop long-term, profitable relationships with customers.

—**Alex Gourlay**, former EVP of Walgreens Boots Alliance

The Metail Economy identifies a critical consumer change that executives ignore at their peril.

—**Miguel Leal**, Global Consumer Marketing Leader (Frito Lay, Kettle, KIND, Cholula) and cofounder of SOMOS Foods

An important and engaging book full of powerful insights and guidance. The *Me*tail paradigm shift affects every business. Bines tells you what to do about it.

—**Ali Velshi**, host of *Velshi* on MSNBC and NBC business correspondent

Every strategic or operational decision must start with your customer, so understanding consumers is critical to business success. Bines lays out a clear and compelling case for a new consumer dynamic and therefore the need for a new operating model. His prescriptions are fresh and direct, and if you hope to stay ahead of the competition, *The Metail Economy* is required reading.

—**Chuck Rubin**, former Chairman and CEO of Michaels, former CEO of Ulta, and former President of Office Depot

If you know Joel, you know he's a no-nonsense expert with a broad and deep understanding of retail and the consumer. His "voice" is loud and clear throughout this book that should be required reading for anyone interested in understanding today's consumer landscape. If you don't know Joel, after reading this book, you will want to.

—**Marc Cooper**, CEO of PJ Solomon

As a designer, it is imperative that I stay ahead of my customers. *The Metail Economy* is by far the best articulation of today's dynamic consumer and the challenges facing every company that serves them. This the most intuitive and relevant book I've ever read on the challenges and, more importantly, the opportunities in retail today. A must-read!

—**Joseph Abboud**, award-winning fashion designer

I've watched Joel deliver remarkable results with companies in every conceivable type of situation with equal parts intelligence, passion, insight, objectivity, and honesty for two decades. He brings the same refreshing clarity and candor to these pages. The insights here will inform and entertain. You don't want to read this book . . . you need to read this book.

—**Fred Crawford**, former CEO and current board member of AlixPartners

I dedicated my professional career to understanding and serving the consumer and can say with certainty that the paradigm shift Bines identifies in *The Metail Economy* is real, urgent, and misunderstood. For those reasons it is essential reading, whether you are just starting your career or leading global firms. The lessons are clear and direct and will absolutely change your thinking.

—**Stephen Sadove**, former Chairman of the National Retail Federation and former Retail & Consumer Executive (Kraft, Bristol-Myers Squibb, Saks Fifth Avenue)

Joel Bines is inspired and inspiring with his book *The Metail Economy*. Joel and his book are helping us to reinvent the world our world needs. Based on his vast experience and pertinent intuitions, Joel Bines helps us to intelligently and significantly upgrade our offers and services.

> —**Stanislas de Quercize**, board member of Christian
> Louboutin and former President and CEO of Cartier
> and Van Cleef & Arpels

If I was ever in need of a 4 a.m. emergency call in retail, it would be to Joel Bines. *The Metail Economy* brilliantly, wittily—and engrossingly—describes the current state of emergency our beloved retail sector is in. *Everyone* should be making the 4 a.m. call right now, but read this first!

> —**Helen David**, former CMO of Harrods

THE METAIL ECONOMY

THE ME TAIL ECONOMY

ECONOMY

6 Strategies for Transforming
Your Business to Thrive in the
Me-Centric Consumer Revolution

JOEL BINES

New York Chicago San Francisco Athens London
Madrid Mexico City Milan New Delhi
Singapore Sydney Toronto

Copyright © 2022 by Joel Bines. All rights reserved. Printed in the United States of America. Except as permitted under the United States Copyright Act of 1976, no part of this publication may be reproduced or distributed in any form or by any means, or stored in a database or retrieval system, without the prior written permission of the publisher.

1 2 3 4 5 6 7 8 9   LCR   26 25 24 23 22 21

ISBN   978-1-264-27463-5
MHID   1-264-27463-7

e-ISBN   978-1-264-27464-2
e-MHID   1-264-27464-5

Library of Congress Cataloging-in-Publication Data
Names: Bines, Joel, author.
Title: The metail economy : 6 strategies for transforming your business to thrive in the me-centric consumer revolution / Joel Bines.
Description: New York : McGraw Hill, [2022] | Includes bibliographical references and index.
Identifiers: LCCN 2021042596 (print) | LCCN 2021042597 (ebook) | ISBN 9781264274635 (hardback) | ISBN 9781264274642 (ebook)
Subjects: LCSH: Consumer behavior. | Consumer satisfaction. | Retail trade—Management. | Organizational change. | Success in business.
Classification: LCC HF5415.32 .B55 2022 (print) | LCC HF5415.32 (ebook) |DDC 658.8/342—dc23/eng/20211109
LC record available at https://lccn.loc.gov/2021042596
LC ebook record available at https://lccn.loc.gov/2021042597

McGraw Hill books are available at special quantity discounts to use as premiums and sales promotions or for use in corporate training programs. To contact a representative, please visit the Contact Us pages at www.mhprofessional.com.

To my parents:
Thank you for allowing me to find me.

To my wife:
Thank you for helping me become me.

To my siblings:
Thank you for understanding me.

To my children:
Thank you for being you.

CONTENTS

FOREWORD

Over my career I have had the opportunity to work with many consultants under various circumstances. Most are smart and can help articulate and build a strategy geared to the need at hand. What sets Joel apart is his innate ability to come at problems like an operator and connect the customer experience into every discussion.

Don't get me wrong. Joel isn't nice (on the job) and working with him isn't exactly what you'd call fun. To Joel, there are no sacred cows and he doesn't mince words. But at the same time, he listens. I mean really listens and seeks to understand. Working with him feels like working with a peer.

I first heard Joel use the word "*Me*tail" over dinner, and frankly my initial reaction was that I was mad that I didn't coin the phrase myself. But it made so much sense that he would be the one to identify this concept and write such a compelling book about what it is and why it matters. Joel has been all about putting customers at the center of the experience since I've known him, whether it was his customers (me and his other clients) or our customers. *Me*tail so perfectly sums up how business leaders must think now and in the future. In today's always connected world, everything from marketing to pricing to products and services must be tailored to the individual. For a retailer, it is no longer just one store with one strategy and one point of view. To compete for today's consumer, it really must be an assortment of one, millions of times over, accessible from anywhere, anytime, and that's only the beginning. What we brand leaders used to call personalization now must take a deeper form, and that's what Joel has so clearly and engagingly captured in this book.

No matter what sort of business you are in, if you hope to compete for consumers, you are, right now, facing your own version of *Me*tail. With each passing year, consumers want more. By absorbing the principles laid out in *The Metail Economy*, you will find a way to deliver.

Marc J. Metrick
Chief Executive Officer
Saks Fifth Avenue, Inc.

INTRODUCTION

Several years ago, I was on a duck-boat tour of Miami with my wife and kids when my cell phone rang. The call was from a "Master of the Universe" investor who suffers no fools, so I sheepishly asked the driver to pull over.

"I'll meet you back at the hotel," I assured my family as I stepped off the vehicle. I gave a wave as the boat rolled into the crystal blue water of Biscayne Bay, and then I turned my attention to the call.

"I need you to figure out what is going on at [let's call it Company X]," the investor said to me without so much as a hello. "And I need to know by the end of the week."

In less than two years since Company X's board of directors shelled out tens of millions to remove the incumbent CEO and replace him with a new CEO and team, the company's revenues had been cratering. Something was seriously wrong.

I have spent my entire career, almost three decades now, working for and with retailers, brands, services firms, and a wide range of other businesses helping to improve performance. I often say that my two core competencies are luck and timing, but if I had to pick two others it would be my let's call it "direct" nature and my ability to rapidly size up an urgent situation and architect a solution. But a week was a short timeline, even for me.

I showed up at Company X's headquarters and was put in a small office where I sifted through data and met with the few executives I could get to talk to me. At one point, I was permitted to tag along with the executive team on a tour of the company's new model store being built in a nearly abandoned mall close to headquarters. The fact that they spent almost the entire tour debating if the lighting was bright enough was a clue that perhaps they weren't aware of the conclusion I was drawing. The situation was more dire than I imagined. The new leadership team had been spending lavishly on a wide range of initiatives; yet revenue had plummeted over 30 percent, and my analysis showed that the company was in real danger of running out of cash.

That Friday afternoon, I finally got an hour on the CEO's calendar. I made my way up to the executive floor, took a deep breath, paused outside the door to his office, considered for one last moment the situation I was about to walk into, and said to myself, "This is going to be a *dumpster fire*."

The CEO and his team were surrounded by yes-men and highly paid consultants, any one of whom could have sounded the alarm. Yet somehow it was up to me—an outsider with just a few days on the ground—to tell them that they were nearly broke and that a major course correction was needed.

The conference room was tense as I walked through my analysis. The exchange got heated as the CEO and his team tried to push back on my numbers, but I stood my ground. Near the end of the meeting, the CEO got up and started pacing. He came back, put both hands on the table and stared right at me for what felt like an hour. The room was totally silent. The air-conditioning was on full blast, yet I could feel the sweat dripping down my back. Finally, he spoke.

"Tell me this," he said, leaving the "you insubordinate jerk" part unsaid, but clear from the tone. "If we stop now, what will we have accomplished?"

Admittedly, I didn't see that one coming and replied with the first thing that came to mind. "I can't answer *that* question," I told him. "But I *can* tell you this: If you do not stop now, you will go down in history as the fastest management team to bankrupt an iconic, profitable, multibillion-dollar company."

Before they could throw me out of the room themselves, I gathered my belongings in silence, grabbed the next elevator down to the cavernous lobby, walked straight to my rental car, and drove away. Less than a month after our meeting, the CEO and his team were all removed. Several years later, the company filed for bankruptcy.

Over the years, I've had time to reflect on this meeting and the broader lessons from the debacle that unfolded at Company X. While many important lessons can be learned, the most important is something I must continue to remind executives to this day: *You are not smarter than your customer.* What puzzles me is why this is something I find myself saying again and again to otherwise talented leaders. Which leads me to this book, which, at its core, is about relationships.

In particular, I am going to drive home the simple-to-read but difficult-to-absorb point that the relationship between your company and your customer will never be the same. Over the past 20 years, there has been a monumental shift that most companies have missed, which, if left unaddressed, can spell disaster.

Whether you are the CEO of a global company or the sole proprietor of a neighborhood store, this book will help you adjust your vision and achieve the clarity necessary to succeed in this *Me*tail economy—an economy made up of highly fragmented, individualized, empowered, and fluid clusters of consumers, or *Me's*, and explained in greater detail later in the book. Nothing like this consumer power shift has ever happened before. But once you see it, you cannot unsee it. You will rethink every aspect of your business strategy. You will have a greater sense of urgency about things you are not even thinking about right now, and less urgency on the issues you think are paramount. In short, I am going to give you the clarity you need to correct course before your ship runs aground.

You've felt something has been off for a while now. Profits are not where they should be; market share is tougher than ever to gain; investments are not paying off. You've been embracing digital, omnichannel, influencer marketing, customer segmentation models and every other buzzword under the sun. But you still are not making meaningful connections with your customers, and you can't seem to put your finger on why.

Until now, company executives like the aforementioned CEO and many others before him have thought of themselves as the anointed ones who get to decide what goods, services, and experiences to provide on what platforms and for what price. Hubris was almost a job requirement for the "merchant princes" of old. Again, I don't blame them, because that's how it worked for millennia. But as this book will show, in this new world, the game has changed completely and forever.

So how did we get here? What caused this change? Most people would say, "It's the internet, silly." Yes, it is because of technology. But it's not technology the way most people think about it. Not the technology that allows us to buy things from our phone while we're lounging in bed. It's not because of Amazon, or Instagram, or TikTok. It's not because of buy online, pick up in store, or one-hour delivery, or digital stylists, or live shopping.

It's not what the technology enables us to do so much as what the technology has given to the consumer: information and access.

This book grows out of my alarm at seeing executives missing the change. My hope is that the following chapters will remove the blinders and let everyone see how companies will never again be the arbiters of choice the way they once were. They will have to adjust every preconceived notion of how they do business to this reality if they wish to succeed. Consumers are the ones setting the agenda. And they now operate outside of the carefully controlled customer experience zones where companies have felt most comfortable.

On these next pages, I will make the case for *Me*tail. Part I provides a brief history and current examples of companies that have struggled to address the new *Me*tail paradigm and some that are on the right path. The three chapters in Part I will show you exactly what *Me*tail means and why it matters.

Then in Part II, I will show you what to do about it by breaking *Me*tail down into a set of six models that can be used to cultivate and serve the consumer in the new *Me*tail reality. Inspired by the four Cs of a diamond—cut, clarity, carat, and color—I call these models the six Cs for success: cost, convenience, category expertise, curation, customization, and community.

Part III will help you to develop self-awareness through the lens of the six Cs, and give you the tools and insights to understand how your organization is viewed and valued by your customers so you can focus your investment, resources, and energies into the right areas in order to maximize your customer relationships in the *Me*tail economy.

My purpose in writing this book is not to be prescriptive, because there is no one-size-fits-all solution. Despite what many business books would have you believe, there is no methodological silver bullet to solve a business problem. Never has been, and never will be. Just as individuals have unique characteristics, so do businesses. Too many business books take a handful of anecdotes and weave them together to manufacture a prescription that no company could possibly replicate. They oversimplify things by forcing solutions into neat frameworks—clean rows of actions that emanate from one central theory. I've spent countless hours unraveling the mistakes made by clients who have twisted themselves into knots trying to put these theories into practice in the real world, and frankly, I'm tired of it.

Like your Me's, your business is like no other. It's as unique as you are and the Me's you serve. Just as no other person without my identical experiences could approach work the way I do, your company has its own DNA but also lessons learned. So, yes, even though I am writing a business book, I am criticizing the genre because most business books are the functional equivalent of my middle-school basketball coach telling me to go home and work on getting taller. As unsexy as it may sound, success requires leveraging your particular set of strengths while being brutally honest about your limitations and weaknesses.

As I tell my clients, you can wish for anything you want, but unless you have a genie in a bottle, accept your limitations as you figure out how to compete in the *Me*tail universe. There are no shortcuts.

My goal is for you to get from the following chapters the important fact that your world has changed and why.

Put plainly, the ultimate takeaway is this: *In today's Metail economy, companies must come to a revised understanding of their relationship with the customer, then rearrange priorities to fund investments that will ensure profitable growth, which after all is the name of the game.* Like a shot of espresso, these next pages are intended to jolt you awake and help you to see the consumer landscape through a new lens. Once you have this clarity, *Me*tail will no longer seem like a problem to solve but the long-awaited opportunity to reimagine, reinvent, and renew your company.

PART I

RETAIL'S REIGN AND THE *ME*TAIL UPRISING

In these next three chapters, I will make the case for a consumer revolution unlike anything that has occurred throughout history. I will trace the origins of consumerism, dating back thousands of years all the way up to today, to put the scope and scale of *Me*tail in context. My intention here is to demonstrate that, in spite of all the models to sell goods and services that have been developed, how humans transacted with one another has remained essentially the same. Whether a consumer was buying a pair of boots from a cobbler circa 1685 or browsing for acid-washed jeans in a suburban shopping mall circa 1985, nothing fundamental about the relationship had changed. Then along came the internet, giving consumers unprecedented access to information, shifting the power into *their* hands.

By the end of Part I, you will understand just how profound this power reversal really is, and the deep implications for your business.

WHEN RETAIL WAS KING

When a customer enters my store, forget me. He is king.

—JOHN WANAMAKER (ICONIC AMERICAN MERCHANT)

The sumptuous shoe on display at the Metropolitan Museum of Art in New York had been worn by King Louis XIV, and it said it all. Featured in the "Camp: Notes on Fashion" exhibition, it was a painstakingly crafted piece of footwear, embellished with a satin bow and a three-inch red heel. Next to this exquisite object was a portrait of the Sun King with his hand on hip, draped in a billowing blue velvet cloak. But I wasn't necessarily thinking about the outrageous campiness of the portrait as I took in those details.

I was more interested in the sheer power that all those luxurious objects signified.

King Louis was the alpha consumer of his day, commanding couturiers, craftsmen, and artisans to make the muddy trek by foot or horse to Versailles from their workshops in Paris, then wait for hours outside his private apartments for the opportunity to show him selections of leather, furs, fabrics, and jewels that would go into the making of his spectacular garb.

In this way, it can be said that King Louis founded the luxury retail industry. While there had always existed some form of retail trade, he established a whole new level of consumerism. He set the kinds of rules and rituals by which fashionistas were to live evermore: Only aristocrats in the king's favor could wear red soles (*wait, you thought Louboutin invented them?*); fashion must change on a strict schedule consisting of two seasons (*hiver* and *été—there were no cruises in his day*); certain fabrics are never to be worn out of season (*where did you think the rule of "no white after Labor Day" came from?*); and wear only the latest styles or be banished from court (*ever been on a middle school playground at recess?*).

But here's the thing: *Today's consumer has more power than the Sun King ever had.*

That's right. History's longest-reigning monarch (many of whose subjects believed the sun and planets literally revolved around him) was more at the mercy of his outfitters than today's consumer, who now possesses access to everything they need to make their own choices about what products and services to buy; where to buy them; how they get bundled, packaged, and delivered; and how, how much, and even when to pay for them.

Sure, Louis had the option of banishing some poor cobbler into obscurity (the *Grand Siècle*'s version of a one-star review). But the power still rested with the designers and craftsmen who decided what fabrics and colors to present to the young *roi*, predetermining the range of choices they offered him. Godlike though he was, even the king of France could not get all he wanted, whenever and however he wanted it. And delivered in an hour? He was lucky if it was delivered in a year. You see, the merchants and service providers of Louis's day were just like all the merchants who came before and for centuries afterward. They alone possessed the power of choice over their customers, who, no matter how powerful, could only choose from the limited selection the merchant was willing to offer them.

And this power dynamic has pretty much been the case before and since . . . until now.

Togas for Sale

I could go even further back to demonstrate how nothing fundamental has changed since humans first got together to trade shells for seeds. There's archaeological evidence of retailing, going back more than 10,000 years, and coins being used in public markets across Asia Minor, Egypt, and ancient Greece as far back as 6000 BCE. By 800 BCE, in ancient Greece, merchants were selling their wares in a public marketplace. We've all heard of the Colosseum in Rome as the place for ruthless entertainment for the masses. But the nearby Trajan's Forum was the Roman equivalent of the outdoor shopping mall, with permanent stalls and shop fronts for artisans selling what they'd crafted in metalwork, leather goods, toga stitching, wineskins, and whatever else a citizen might need or want almost 3,000 years ago.

For centuries thereafter, artisans and tradespeople set up shop in the streets and in market squares. If you wanted to buy boots, you would head to the nearest town's "Cobbler's Row" to have them made, likely right around the corner from where the milliners (hatmakers) set up shop. That basic system of retail still exists in developing economies like Vietnam's, where citizens shopping for every electronic item from televisions to air conditioners head over to Hai Ba Trung Street in Hanoi. Even today in New York City, for example, jewelry shoppers can take their chances in the Diamond District on 47th Street (where, incidentally, I bought my wife's engagement ring in 1992).

From Main Street to Superstore

"Mom-and-pops" at first proliferated throughout the United States in the form of pharmacies and general stores selling everything from toys to farm equipment, liniments, fabric for making dresses, and whatever else settlers needed for their daily lives. This collection of retailers on the side streets, as well as general stores on Main Street, gave way first to mail-order and catalog shopping and then to the suburban mall in the mid-1950s, when architect Viktor David Grunbaum built the first enclosed shopping center in North America. Again, it was nothing particularly new. He was trying to re-create the kind of communal gathering space—with shopping, art, and entertainment—that existed back home in the European market square.

These locations quickly became a commercial oasis in the cultural desert of the American suburb, the place to go on weekends to see a movie, eat in the food court, or browse Strawberry's or Waldenbooks. For a period of time, the mall became the center of the universe in terms of consumer culture, and in 1986, it was even selected as one of the Top 50 Wonders[1] that revolutionized the lives of consumers. Yet in spite of the "this-changes-everything" new-retail-model hysteria, all this changing of locations and store type *still* did nothing to change the dynamic between the customer and the store. You bought whatever was on offer, or nothing at all.

Next came the big-box stores, where efficiency and well-stocked shelves trumped the personal touch of neighborhood stores. In 1962, Walmart started this revolution in store format when it opened its first location in Rogers, Arkansas. As much as people enjoyed the mall walk, many consumers preferred the one-stop shop, where they could find what they needed, typically for less than on Main Street.

So from one perspective, it has been one disruption after another but, in spite of that, never an actual revolution. Whether you were circling your local mall's giant lot, vying for a coveted parking space near one of the anchor stores like Filene's or JCPenney, or driving to the nearest big city to do some retail therapy on a Miracle Mile or Fifth Avenue, you *still* had to come to the retailer to buy whatever wares it had chosen to make available for you.

Some of these store models were more pleasurable or convenient or both. Some were none of the above. If you're old enough, maybe you remember a time when, for example, if you lived in a small town like Buck Creek, Indiana, and you needed a snowblower, you had to drive to the nearest Sears or Toro dealer 40 miles away, braving whiteouts on the freeway, because it was the only place you could get one, and you had at best a choice of three, maybe four models. The point is that the companies selling to consumers owned the power in the relationship. Anyone old enough to remember some of the retailers mentioned on these pages must surely remember feeling, "I really wish I didn't have to buy this thing from this place, but I don't have a choice."

This power dynamic has been the one constant through line of buyer-seller iterations for millennia. Humans bought or traded for items they desired from other humans who had them, with the consumer meeting the retailers where they were, not the other way around. It was the companies that determined what was available when, to whom, and for how much. They called the shots.

Fight the Power

Except, as you may have noticed—and I'm talking pre-pandemic—some of the biggest retail names in the global consumer market have been struggling to stay in business. The pandemic accelerated the trend, but the cull has been a long time coming. This is despite companies scrambling to increase their online presence, providing an endless array of other services, chatbots, personalization, and whatever other offering they can think of to keep up with the Jones.comses. But how can this be? If it's just about adding new models or digital investments, then why are so many retail, restaurant, and other consumer-facing businesses struggling to survive? Put simply, it is because businesses have largely missed the point.

Consumer expectations began to evolve in the early-to-mid-1990s, when eBay, Amazon, and other pioneers launched the first wave of digital retail. (I discuss this evolution in Chapter 2.) But too many consumer companies are operating under the false assumption that the difference was the ability to buy goods and services online. As you will see, this is not the point. The key change arose through the power of information, with consumers using technology as research and connection tools before making their purchasing decisions. With ever more information becoming available, and with the concomitant power to disseminate their own thoughts and feelings to one another, consumers outgrew and rejected the age-old company-customer relationship and began behaving in ways companies still can't quite comprehend. Around 2010, the winds of change could already be felt in erratic demand and ineffective marketing campaigns, but even as the digital space became less chaotic and more sophisticated, companies failed to recognize that the consumer had taken control, and this failure to see the power shift continues to this day.

Moving Targets

This change has created the consumer model that underpins the concept of *Me*tail. Instead of being the reliable demographic clusters we're used to targeting, consumers have fragmented and then fragmented again into what I refer to as "Me's." Me's are constantly regrouping and changing according to social trends, identity politics, personal whims, and even time of day, resulting in the atomization of traditional demographic categories into factions of one, or a few, where individuals flow in and out of clusters unpredictably and, more importantly, can associate themselves with multiple clusters at the same time and change their associations over time.

Me's are not static. I may be your target consumer at a place and moment in time and may not be so in the next instant, and if you do not capture me in that instant, you may never capture me, because I will be someone else's consumer, for a time.

One of my mentors, Fred Crawford, along with his coauthor, futurist Ryan Mathews, first identified this concept in their 2003 book, *The Myth of Excellence*,[2] with the concept of the "instavidual," the consumer who might be satisfied with something as basic as an Egg McMuffin at 7 a.m. but "catch that same individual at 7 p.m. and an acceptable meal looks like a filet mignon and a double extra-dry martini at Morton's of Chicago."

This multifaceted, nonstatic, nonlinear Me is precisely why the old model is doomed to fail in the *Me*tail economy. Now it's all about a Me whose wants, desires, whims, and needs vary from year to year, month to month, week to week, and day to day—even second to second. It is now up to companies to meet them where they are, not the other way around.

I'll dedicate more time to defining Me's in Chapter 3. But my overall point is this: The simplest way to think about *Me*tail is as the absolute democratization of consumerism. For evidence that this is happening, look no further than Facebook, which has 71 customizable gender options for users, and counting. Whatever your politics, and however you feel about this, how people identify themselves today goes way beyond binary gender, age, ethnicity, socioeconomic background, education, or nationality.

In a chat with a reporter on the instant-messaging platform Discord, Facebook CEO Mark Zuckerberg noted this trend as it relates to the challenges that his own industry's traditional gate-keepers are facing: "If you look at the grand arc here, what's really happening is individuals are getting more power and more opportunity to create the lives and jobs that they want."[3]

We live in a world of extreme individualism where consumer voices have grown loud and influential, so you could be forgiven for feeling dizzy right now.

The Second-Oldest Profession

Despite the shift that has taken place, the consumer's never-ending desire to consume remains as strong as ever. Even during the pandemic and related social and economic crises, retail sales in the United States rose 6.9 percent to $4.04 trillion from $3.78 trillion the year before, according to an analysis of the latest US Department of Commerce figures. So hardly a death knell for retail.

Yet the vast majority of this growth has gone to the few companies that understand the changing consumer. To an extent, the headline growth number is masking the challenges of tens of thousands of consumer-facing companies.

Retail survived a global pandemic and will continue to survive unless some other apocalyptic event forces the entire global population to live off the grid, with people growing their own vegetables and hunting rabbits for stew. Even then, we'd need to barter with someone for seeds and perhaps a stock pot, and the cycle would continue. Selling goods and services has been in a constant state of renewal since the earliest days of commerce. Yes, artisans were disrupted by merchants, who were disrupted by bazaars and spice-route traders. True, pushcarts disrupted stand-alone stores. Sure, the Sears Roebuck catalog of 1893 disrupted the first era of brick-and-mortar retail. Absolutely, malls disrupted the town square; superstores and category killers disrupted the local five-and-dime. And Amazon, the great disrupter, has disrupted, well, almost every consumer-facing business (or will soon). But each time one of these iterations of retail becomes obsolete, another takes its place. There really is no imaginable scenario where humans won't be making some form of transaction to fulfill a want, a need, or a desire.

Which is why, when the business page headlines lament yet another store closure, with dire forecasts about the end of retail, it makes my eyes roll. Of course, you could be forgiven for thinking major sectors of the industry are in their final death throes. The average person reading the news might naturally come to the mistaken conclusion that there will be no more brick-and-mortar stores in the very near future. And if you happen to work in a consumer-facing company that is struggling, what is happening now must feel apocalyptic. Thousands of physical stores shuttered as people sheltered in place during the COVID-19 pandemic, with more than 12,000 retail stores closing in the United States alone, not to mention all the restaurants, gyms, and other consumer-oriented locations.[4] Meanwhile, e-commerce made up almost 16 percent of retail sales in the United States by the end of 2020—a substantial jump from ~11 percent in 2019.[5]

So yes, there has been pain. Other than groceries, toilet paper, and PPE equipment, people didn't buy a whole lot in the first few months of the pandemic. It's not like you needed to purchase a new wardrobe to sit on your sofa and binge-watch *Tiger King*. Several fast-fashion retail chains filed for bankruptcy, as well as mid-market and high-end department stores, gourmet food companies, restaurants, bakeries, and brands.

Even before the onset of the global pandemic, one major news outlet even forecast "The Death of Clothing."[6] But again, we should be careful of the headlines about retail's demise. As an operator and consultant who has devoted his working life to the consumer economy, I am especially pained by these headlines because they suggest old-line companies might as well throw up their hands rather than find creative solutions. Adding to the confusion, much of what is written today about struggling consumer businesses attributes the struggle to the rise of e-commerce, but that misses the point.

Kill or Cure

Contrary to the hysteria, consumer sales are, in fact, growing. Consider the fact that by the end of 2021, people shifted from hoarding hand sanitizer to nesting, home improvement, outdoor experiences and even freshening up that wardrobe. And it wasn't only the online retailers that benefited from consumers' pent-up demand. Brick-and-mortar stores also saw traffic from individuals escaping their cabin fever and shopping for everything from cars (new and used) to fishing rods to gaming consoles and everything in between.

I remain a firm believer in the future of brick-and-mortar stores. Here's why: Recent store closures are actually a sign that some of those companies are on the right path. No industry could have sustained the kind of overcapacity that US retailers have been carrying, and the fact that the industry's leaders are finally waking up to this reality is healthy. Overexposure to high-priced real estate has been a huge drain, and the pandemic helped to accelerate a market correction that had already been under way.

The pandemic forced a few necessary adjustments, but much of it was done in a scrappy way. The time that businesses would have normally taken to study (forever) what changes to make was not available. The problem now is, these much-needed changes introduced new complexities and costs into businesses, making it even harder to figure out what to do as we unwind from the pandemic.

Mass market retailers, in particular, "won" the pandemic, if you can call it a victory. Target added more than $15 billion in sales in 2020, more than the sales growth of the prior 11 years combined.[7] Costco, Walmart, and some (but not all) big-box stores also saw impressive growth.

It's instructive to look at Target because it would be all too easy to think the company just got lucky. Target outperformed because its moves were intentional and played into its corporate strategy—not surprisingly, because it was the only major retailer whose strategy explicitly made the sort of changes necessary to compete in the *Me*tail economy. Around 2017, when Brian Cornell took over as CEO. Target decided "It's about the customer, stupid!" and began to think deeply about all the many ways customers might want to shop. Target focused its investments on consumer benefits and invested billions. And while of course Target could not have predicted 2020, its focused investment paid off and provided consumers what they needed at precisely the right moment in history.

Take same-day delivery and curbside pickup, for example. Target was well ahead of its brick-and-mortar competition in offering both, and with a store within 10 miles of three-quarters of customers, its same-day delivery nearly tripled, and its curbside pickup exploded as well. In troubling times, with media images of people elbowing each other out of the way to buy the last bottle of Clorox on the shelf, Target gave its customers the assurance that their needs would be met safely and efficiently because Target was ready: The company had already invested in making its 1,900+ stores capable of local fulfillment.

Doubled Down

Along with its digital capabilities, Target had also been investing billions in its physical stores to improve them visually, increase customer friendliness, and also improve them functionally to create local distribution hubs that are a kind of hybrid between in-person and online shopping.

"A few years ago, everyone said stores were obsolete," Cornell told *Forbes* in an interview. "We took the other path, not because it was our opinion—it was what consumers were telling us."[8]

Target invested in its associates to ensure that all facets of its customer service—from buy online/pick up in store to face-to-face interactions with customers—was spot on. Retail workers who traditionally toiled in low-pay, high-stress jobs were suddenly getting better salaries and training. They were also offered additional sick leave, child care, and education benefits. Other retailers offer elements of this, but Target understood how all these elements played together: the associate, the customer, the store, and the technology.

Target made smart, strategic customer-centric acquisitions to add to capabilities it knew the customer wanted, instead of, for example, making random acquisitions of e-commerce companies as some of its competitors did. Target's contrarian approach, especially its decision to double down on physical stores, got punished in the stock market when Cornell began rolling it out. But he was proved right with increasing sales and market share even before the pandemic hit. Of course, its stores carry the essentials that largely home-bound consumers needed to get through the crisis, but so did many others, and Target outperformed them all.

I am not suggesting that Target's tactics should be the model for everyone. Instituting curbside order fulfillment or buying a last-mile delivery company may be an inappropriate strategy for your business, and you may not have the size or financial resources to invest the billions that Target did. But Target *is* a model for how retailers can totally reorient themselves around *Me*tail. Its success started with a complete shift in perspective to understand that the consumer is in charge and that it is the consumer who dictates to the retailer, despite what the industry and capital markets were saying. Target persisted because it paid close attention to the demands of its consumers. That the pandemic dramatically accelerated its success is hardly the point.

As I will remind you, there is no single, standardized recipe for *Me*tail. By the end of this book, you will have formulated your own plan, based on an awareness of your strengths and weaknesses and what you can offer to your particular set of customers. But the one thing you should all share is a sense of urgency. There is no more time to waste on misdirected spending priorities or half-hearted commitments to trendy buzzwords.

We've reached a critical juncture, and so much depends on the survival of these businesses. More than 100 million Americans make their living in some facet of the consumer economy. Hundreds of millions more do so around the world. Understanding and acting on the concepts in this book will mean the difference between a company's future success and more store closures, job losses, and shareholder pain.

This reckoning has been years in the making, but recent events have laid bare the weaknesses in retail all the more. Pre-COVID, we had maybe another 5 to 10 years to address the change. Post-COVID, it's more like 5 to 10 minutes. But before you go into panic mode, pull back and look at this moment within the context of the full sweep of history. A rebirth *is* possible.

Again, that old cycle—the fall of the old and the rise of the new—has always existed. Humans have always found new ways to go to market with an array of goods and services. Commerce has always found a way. The point is that dating back millennia, the company's basic relationship to the consumer has remained the same.

Then along came the internet, which did change everything, but not for the reasons many of you thought, and some of you still think. *Me*tail is the great *consumer* revolution because consumers have stormed the castle, and it is finally *they* who reign over the marketplace as kings and queens with absolute power.

Sorry Sun King, but the Me's rule.

2

THEN ALONG CAME THE INTERNET

It is not the strongest of the species that survives . . .
It is the one that is the most adaptable to change.

—CHARLES DARWIN

Toward the end of the twentieth century, a kind of virtual bazaar took form with online bidding for goods via The Source, MicroNet, Onsale.com, and, of course, eBay. These platforms were like private auctions attended by the early adopters, mostly computer whizzes with the patience to endure slow dial-up connections and navigate the bits and bytes of computer coding to access deals.

Brick-and-mortar companies felt they could safely ignore these fringe shoppers. Anything happening on the internet back then was considered too "out there" to take seriously. And even when people started paying attention during the first dot-com bubble, the burst at the beginning of the new millennium left most executives feeling vindicated. I can just imagine some of them high-fiving each other for being so smart, as the black-and-white-spotted sock-puppet dog, the mascot for Pets.com (that too-early iteration of Chewy), became the symbol of so many online retail failures.

It's not as if these internet innovators were wrong. In fact, virtually every dot-com 1.0 idea has become a part of today's consumer economy. Webvan, for instance, an online grocery delivery business that delivered products to peoples' homes within a half-hour window of their choosing, was a great concept. But it became yet another symbol of the dot-com-bubble excess, filing for bankruptcy in 2001 after spending more than a billion dollars. The company was right about where the world was going, but wrong about how long it would take to get there, and the consumer's adoption rate wasn't fast enough to keep up with Webvan's spending.

Then along came Amazon.

In 1994, Jeff Bezos had quit his lucrative job at an investment firm on Wall Street and traveled across the country to Seattle, writing his business plan along the way. He had a hunch that there was vast, untapped potential for selling stuff via the internet, so in 1995, he set up a small office in his garage. After successfully beta-testing his site with 300 of his closest friends, Bezos went live with an online bookstore.

In less than a month, with no press and little in the way of promotion, Amazon.com began selling books not just across the United States but in 45 countries, reaching $20,000 a week in sales. The company went public in 1997 and, two years after that, had established itself as a leader in e-commerce, even as skeptics doubted its ability to ever make money. But Amazon continued to grow and diversify into music, videos, electronics, toys, and then every category imaginable. Its sales climbed from $510,000 in 1995 to more than a billion by the end of the 1990s, and almost $400 billion today.

Meanwhile many business executives continued to congratulate themselves for being smart enough not to fall for the internet music man. Others simply buried their heads in the brick-and-mortar dust, convinced that, whether they were selling furniture, clothes, or shoes, their consumers "would never buy my category online." And until around 2005, it was largely true. In fact, the nineties to mid-2000s were a good time to be a brick-and-mortar retailer: It was the era of conspicuous consumption with yet more stores and malls opening—a boom that lasted until the financial crisis and recession hit in 2008. At that point, e-commerce represented just a tiny sliver of sales for most products. So, to be fair, things were happening so gradually that the signals were easy to miss.

Pushcart Epiphany

During this period I was aware of the transformational role technology was playing in the consumer marketplace, but it hadn't struck me with full force until I went on a family vacation to Peru. We tried the local food and checked out all the cultural spots and places of natural beauty. In an area called the Sacred Valley of the Incas, we visited a crowded market selling every Peruvian curio you could imagine. We came across a small stall that sold bags of fine Peruvian salt. Back then, gourmet salt was becoming a thing, but this stuff was truly special because of its rarity. It comes from Maras, a town in southeastern Peru known for its thousands of individual salt pools flecking the surrounding hillsides.

There was just one little problem as I saw it: how to carry plastic bags of a powdery white substance hand-labeled "salt"into the

United States. My wife and I were amused at the thought—but also unwilling to argue the optics of a bag of white powder being carried in from South America with United States customs.

As we stood discussing a possible solution, my youngest piped up, "Why don't you just buy it on Amazon when we get home?"

That was my V8 moment. I was already a regular Amazon customer for things like electronics and books, and well aware that you could get many other items on the website, but it had never occurred to me that I could order up such a rare and special product from an exotic corner of the world with a couple of clicks. Yet, sure enough, when I got home and searched Amazon, there it was.

Executives responded differently to the threat of Amazon's ubiquity, reach, convenience, and efficiency, but all too often they just hoped it would go away. And while Amazon itself is not the revolution, it is endemic of the growing power being vested in the Me's. That early dismissal cost companies precious time to raise the bulwarks against this coming revolution. Companies had about a 10-year window to invest in the build-out of a more Me-oriented infrastructure, but by and large, they missed it.

No Going Back

Countless businesses continued to believe they were surrounded by moats that would protect them against digital disruption. But consider as just one example what has happened to traditional taxis and car service companies since the emergence of such ride-sharing apps as Uber, Lyft, Ola, Didi, and others. At first, ride-sharing triggered an outcry among taxi and limousine services as they saw their business being disrupted, and they did what most other legacy businesses had done through the ages—turn to their politicians. And at first, their method worked. Uber had to shut down or curtail service in many cities around the world and faced numerous other legal challenges to its business. But here's the thing about the *Me*tail economy: Once you introduce something Me-centric, there's no going back.

While Uber got sued and paid fines, its customers rose up in support of ride-sharing, because it made their lives so much easier. While politicians and local municipalities considered how to stop Uber, it became more popular than ever—and not only is it not going away, but it's become a verb.

Nothing can protect entrenched players when Me's want what they want. A few years ago, the CEO of a haircutting chain boasted to me that his business couldn't be disrupted because every state and municipality had its own laws and requirements, be that a particular level of training, mandated certifications, and the like. Now you'll find Squire, the "Uber of haircuts," and Shortcut, which delivers hairstyling to your home or office, and multiple other versions of the same Me-centric styling service. In fact, I challenge you to name a product or service that used to require an appointment and visit to a physical location that is now not available at home or office or virtually through the click of an app. Until just a couple of years ago, this individualized and on-demand consumption was unfathomable—unless, of course, you were paying attention.

There is no safe haven from the *Me*tail consumer no matter what business you are in. Sure, there are customs and conventions as well as history, prior investment, infrastructure, and maybe even laws that could or should create challenges, but your Me's and your digitally native rivals don't care. If there's a chance to be the next Amazon, Lyft, or Grubhub, it's worth the risk. Yes, your digital rivals are funded by a mountain of cash from investors who may not care about long-term value creation, but rather care more about unicorn-level valuations and exits. Yes, they will lose hundreds of millions or billions collectively, and yes, most will indeed go the way of those late last-century dot–come-ons from version 1.0. So what? What we are witnessing is the creative destruction wrought by Me's, delivered by companies willing to challenge preconceived notions about how to serve them. Complaining about the unfairness of it all may be satisfying, but it will get you nowhere.

This generation of business builders—your competitors—are rule breakers and risk takers, just like their *Me*tail customers. They defy conventional thinking. Ask any optical retailer a couple of years ago if it were possible to buy eyeglasses without ever visiting an optician to update a prescription, and the answer would have been an emphatic *no* with all the practical reasons why not. Tell that to Warby Parker and its prescription check app. Never go to a gas station and pump your own gas again, having gas delivered to your car? Impossible! Tell that to Fuelster, Filld, Yoshi, and Booster. Well, fine, but you can't move a carwash, right? I haven't visited a single carwash since discovering MobileWash, the on-demand app for car washing. This fragmentation of the formerly asset-intensive distribution of goods and services plays perfectly into the desire of Me's for what they want in the moment they want it at the place they want it.

On-demand goods and services are just the tip of the iceberg. Once people learned that they could access never-before-heard-of amounts of information and could share that information with each other, consumers began to behave differently. Suddenly, demographic groups who could previously be thought of as acting like schools of fish and marketed to accordingly began acting more as individuals, making buying decisions based on what other consumers were saying, not what companies were. In simple terms, technology-enabled consumers took over the marketplace. Digital natives and a few forward-thinking companies realized this change in who was actually in control. But most legacy businesses have remained hidebound, or they've confused tactics for transformation because that has always been by far the most comfortable position.

Even as companies began to feel the effects of this relationship shift in the form of flagging sales and profits, they mostly attributed the cause of their woes to Amazon's popularity for traditional retail and to other disrupters in other consumer spaces. Instead of stepping back to examine what was really going on, businesses mostly spent the past two decades making costly moves in the wrong direction, as though they were boxing blindfolded. Worse than the wasted money is the wasted time.

Macy's Monolith

Macy's was among many companies that decided size and scale was the answer for a consumer business, and it went all-in to consolidate its sector. It had grown from a dry goods store founded in the mid-1800s selling to mill workers in Haverhill, Massachusetts, to a massive physical aggregator of goods, with close to 600 stores, 130,000 employees, and $28 billion in revenues by 2014. There was a time when middle-class consumers pretty much had to shop at Macy's because it dominated in just about every category, from furnishings to fashion. It wasn't a monopoly to be sure, but it was the place you were most likely to find what you were searching for under one roof, whether you were shopping for a gift, looking for trendy fall boots, registering for a wedding, or buying a new mattress.

The consolidation began in the mid-1990s, long before Amazon was anything more than a river. Through acquisition, Macy's had accumulated a heterogenous collection of regional brands, and for a time it continued to operate that way. But then, mainly in the interests of efficiency and streamlining costs, Macy's started phasing out the individual identities of its banners. It would be much simpler to operate as one company with one brand, the thinking went. But it was a company-first mindset that ignored what the customer might want.

Long-time customers disliked the makeovers, as did the associates. "There were moments when I was walking into places like Davison's [in Atlanta] or Bullock's in Southern California, fearing I might get pelted with rotten tomatoes," recalled one former senior executive at Macy's who had been closely involved with nine consolidations.

The day Davison's changed its signage to Macy's, the executive (whom we'll call Jim) overheard a conversation among three women at the entrance to the store. They were confused.

"I could have sworn there was a Davison's here," one of them said. Trying to be helpful, Jim explained to them that it was Davison's, but that it was undergoing a rebranding.

"You're changing it to a New York store?!" one of the women exclaimed.

"But what y'all want to do that for? We're in Atlanta!"

(*What y'all want to do that for, indeed.*)

Of course, it wasn't only the signage that changed. As consolidation and cost cutting did not deliver enough profit, homogenization set in largely because that's what inevitably follows this strategy—providing differentiation is costly. When Macy's started homogenizing its I. Magnin stores—where well-heeled women formerly shopped for their designer gowns—Macy's merchandized as if I. Magnin were a middle-market store, buying sweaters, skirts, and dresses in bulk, turning off I. Magnin's core customers, leaving too much unsold inventory and adding promotions, all deadly to a store with a high-end image.

It was a similar story at Bullock's in Los Angeles. Employees there took great pride in their store, and they knew their customers well, but one of the first cost-focused moves from Macy's headquarters was to purge their six buyers, sending Bullock's and the more high-end Bullock's Wilshire into a steady decline, because there was a complete disconnect between those making the merchandising decisions for those locations and the wants of their Me's. At the time though, Me's lacked any power to do anything about it. "Customers can take it or leave it" was the attitude in many boardrooms pursuing the consolidate and homogenize strategy.

But who can blame them? From the late 1990s until the Great Recession, Macy's did indeed benefit from the cost savings driven by homogenization along with that period's booming consumption. Macy's was making too much money to see the trouble brewing on the horizon. Me's were angry, but they had no recourse.

In July 2005, Federated (Macy's parent company) announced, based on the apparent success of converting its own regional brands to the Macy's name, it would do the same to the 330 department stores formerly owned by the May Company. Powerful regional brands would again fall. The iconic Marshall Fields of Chicago would be no more. Film critic Roger Ebert voiced the sentiment of thousands of heartbroken Chicagoans when he wrote under the genius headline, "Plowing Fields Won't Grow Business": "I thought the day would never come. I am looking at my Field's charge card, which I have cut up into tiny pieces. They look like the color of money."[1]

One by one they fell: Filene's, Kaufmann's, Famous-Barr, Foley's, Robinsons-May, The Jones Store, Meier & Frank, Hecht's, L. S. Ayres, Strawbridge & Clothier . . . People were vocal about their disappointment, vowing they'd never shop in the rebranded stories again. But pre-internet, there was really no way for those voices to find other voices and so on. This strategy continued to work, and until about a decade ago, it was actually a good time to be the biggest mall-based anchor in the country.

Correcting Course

Macy's did eventually recognize the shift to *Me*tail and have been making impressive moves to correct course. They have been adding smaller stores and more localized merchandising, entering the off-price market, doubling-down on meeting their consumers where they are, and developing "customer experience" technologies, like an interactive fragrance display. Noticing that its consumers search by scent categories when they are buying online but by brand when they are in the store, it developed a digital alternative to replicate the online experience in stores through an interactive fragrance display that allows shoppers to identify their favorite notes and fragrance family. As they pick up one of the bottles on display, a digital interface offers more information about the brand and suggests other scents to match their preferences.

Macy's is also incorporating augmented reality into its beauty department through its mobile app and in select stores, so that consumers can find that perfect shade of red lipstick virtually, on whatever platform they prefer to shop. During the pandemic, when customers were not able to physically try on shades (and may never physically do it again), the timing of this digital and physical store experience was fortuitous.

Macy's has also been right sizing. The company closed 30 locations in 2020, with plans to shutter another 45 in 2021, part of a three-year plan to close 125 stores by 2023. The key question is, was the shift to Metail recognized soon enough and has the course correction been significant enough. The sales decline has been steep. Macy's had $30 billion in annual sales at the time of the 2005 May-Federated merger (inflation-adjusted, that's nearly $40 billion in today's dollars), but Macy's did only $24.6 billion in sales in 2019, the final full year before the pandemic, and only about $18 billion in a pandemic-impacted 2020. But their actions in the past few years have been intentional and well thought through.

Will these shifts in approach—scaling down and attempting to meet their Me's where they are—be enough? I am not in the prediction business, but I will offer my view that it is not too late. If Macy's has understood the premise of this book, then I like its chances.

Opportunity Within Crisis

Scale *can* be an effective competitive strategy, but not at the expense of the customer. Scale must be a customer value, not a company value, and Me's are not stupid: They know the difference. Every day, I see evidence that despite the tsunami that's rolling over them, many global consumer-oriented company leaders are unable to let go of the notion that they know what's best for their consumers.

The challenge is real, but do not think that the game is over and that Amazon and digitally native direct-to-consumer companies have won. Yes, Amazon is the most supersized of them all, and it's a formidable competitor because its business is fully designed from the customer backward. And yet Amazon's scale is also your opportunity.

Now is the perfect time for nimble action to chip away at Amazon's market dominance. We saw some chinks in its armor early in the pandemic, when it put its Prime members—who pay $119 a year for the privilege of fast and reliable order fulfillment—on waitlists for groceries and other necessities. During what should have been Amazon's moment to shine, with 90 percent of the population under stay-at-home orders, the company's supply chain got overwhelmed, and rivals entered the breach.

Globally, Amazon is also facing competition from regional e-commerce players, including Coupang in South Korea, Mercadolibre in South America, Jumia in various African countries, and Tokopedia in Indonesia. Global Me's may reject the amorphous mass that is Amazon in favor of these businesses that can better serve their more localized needs. Meanwhile, many Me's in the Western world—where Amazon does, in fact, dominate—are only mostly loyal via the inertia of the ecosystem. Find a way to dislocate Me's from that ecosystem, and they will be yours.

3

THE QUANTUM CONSUMER REVOLUTION

We're still in the first minutes of the first day of the internet revolution.
—SCOTT D. COOK, COFOUNDER OF INTUIT

There's a scene in an episode of the NBC sitcom *Superstore* where management of the Cloud Nine company decides to offer customers free personal-shopping services, readying purchases for pickup within 30 minutes of placing an order. The shoppers roll up to the front of the store in their vehicles and pop open the trunk, and the store staffers load in the boxes and bags to the shoppers' exact specifications.

The orders fly in for this curbside service, and comic havoc ensues. The characters run around the Cloud Nine store in a panic, zipping across the aisles, accumulating thousands of steps on their Fitbits as they rush to fill orders as random and small as a box of thumbtacks, or as cumbersome and heavy as a refrigerator (a customer asks why it's taking so long as the camera cuts to an older employee making no headway as she struggles to push the appliance out of the store). In a later scene, one of the characters gets felled by an SUV in a hit-and-run as she tries to load an overlooked box of wineglasses. Sitting in his office, oblivious to the strife this new offering has caused employees, the manager looks at the huge jump in the number of online orders filled and decides to offer the same service within 20 minutes.

The episode is hilarious except, perhaps, to those of you who are living through this kind of retail nightmare as we speak (especially if you've had to launch "buy online, pick up in store" systems at warp speed due to the pandemic). The Cloud Nine scenario was scripted for the sake of comedy, but it exemplifies the kinds of backflips many traditional companies have been doing as they attempt to make sense of their consumer-facing businesses in the Digital Age.

No one is laughing inside the real world of a struggling retail business. Whether they're big-box chains, high-end department stores, custom shirtmakers, or restaurants, airlines, or any other consumer business, companies of all stripes have been scrambling to meet their customers' changing expectations and, life being stranger than fiction, with mostly comedic results.

It's the Power Inversion, Silly

So what really happened? What's the underlying cause of this turmoil? The answer goes to the core of this book, and it affects every person working in a consumer-oriented business: There's been a revolution: *Over the past 20 years, there has been a full inversion of power in the relationship between consumers and companies.*

Coming full circle, we have finally arrived at our "this-changes-everything moment." This time everything *has* changed, and it's not going back to the way it was. In a fundamental departure from the way the marketplace has been functioning for millennia, the power has shifted *entirely* from company to consumer. Never again will companies control the narrative. Me's insist on being treated as individuals because they have seen the wizard behind the old merchant/consumer curtain. Armed with powerful new information and access, they righteously rebel against homogeneity. They expect their desires to be fulfilled and their needs to be met.

It's time to accept that you are no longer in charge. You no longer get to decide what, where, or how your customers buy things. Your customers have fractured into tribes of one, which, again, I call Me's, and they exist in this new landscape I call *Me*tail. Any company that wants to sell to customers profitably and over the long term must acknowledge and solve this new paradigm of *Me*tail, which is made up of an almost infinite number of individual *Me*'s. These Me's are dictating the terms, and you must accept and embrace this shift in order to compete.

The Me's Have It

Let me explain how, exactly, this power inversion plays out:

The *Me*tail consumers—armed with computers, tablets, smartphones, smartwatches, the metaverse, and each other—have revolted against the very foundational principle of retail, taking over control of product narratives and appropriating the keys to all the storerooms. These emancipated consumers are no longer beholden to companies to create the story of what's on trend and then "present" selections within a set of boundaries (a catalog, a store, a website, a menu, etc.), because as a result of the digital consumer revolution, consumers can create their own stories, and their self-centric demands and buying habits are beyond the ability of companies to categorize or predict. Anyone in the business of selling to consumers must pause and take this in.

As shown when I reviewed the sweep of retail's evolution in Chapters 1 and 2, there have been countless disruptions to the industry. Retail history books are littered with so-called revolutionary moments. And although they did change things, those revolutionary moments never changed the underlying dynamic—which is the exchange of money for goods, controlled by the people with the goods. But this *Me*tail revolution is cataclysmic. Me's have been freed. We now live in a world where a housewife in North Carolina who can't find wholesome clothes for her daughter can connect with a Chinese factory on Alibaba, get her vision of smocked dresses made to spec, sell the extras to like-minded moms on Facebook, and eventually start her own business called Lolly Wolly Doodle. (Yes, it's a real company.)

It bears repeating that what's truly different is not that consumers can buy a muffin tin on Amazon, or a vintage lamp shade on eBay, or a custom mask on Etsy while sitting in their pajamas at home. In other words, this is not about e-commerce. E-commerce is just commerce, as it's been practiced for millennia. This *Me*tail metamorphosis is the complete agency that humankind has been given as a result of the *Me*tail Age.

Google Empowerment

Digital technology has been transformational in ways we are only just beginning to grasp, affecting so many consumer businesses.

Take wellness, for example. We are now our own wellness advocates through the volumes of information about diseases, symptoms, and treatments. For better or worse as far as doctors are concerned, we now walk into our annual checkup armed with detailed knowledge, some of it relevant, some of it not. But just think about how this changes the dynamic between the average person and those who have heretofore been viewed as "in charge" of your health. It forces medical practitioners to be more transparent with you about what they do and do not know. It opens the door to a conversation about alternative treatments and, above all, punctures the myth that the doctor is all powerful.

To take another example, consider the process of buying or selling a home. Now you can go online and check for yourself the comparative prices in your neighborhood or go to a site that crunches data for you about which realtors in the area have the best experience and track record for your type of property. You have the hard facts and analysis from multiple online sources, so you no longer have to rely on the self-promotion you see on the local billboards or written across the for-sale sign on your neighbor's front lawn. Heck, you don't even need a Realtor anymore—not even for physical showings, with the new showing apps permeating the market. The same goes for your investment portfolio. With a little research and practice, if you are so inclined, you now have the ability to make stock picks that are just as or almost as educated as your investment advisor's picks. There is a long and growing list of things in our lives over which we now have full agency, for better or worse. The point is that *Me*tail is everywhere you look.

We can all be experts with Google. It's hard for my kids to imagine what it was like when we didn't have information right at our fingertips. We can settle an argument about who hit the most home runs in the 2018 World Series in seconds by whipping out our iPhones. But there was a time when seeking out some of the most basic information required a lot more legwork, literally.

From Microfiche to Instagram

It's easy to take for granted the information access we currently have. But I cannot overstate how profoundly and fundamentally this changes everything for your business. To put it in context, let's teleport back just a few decades. Up until the mid-1990s, before the internet became accessible to most households, most information was distributed and consumed asynchronously. People learned about products because they saw an ad on a bill-board or in a magazine, heard about them on the radio, or saw them on one of three network television stations. The 1950s housewife used to buy Ivory soap because that's what was adver-tised on the commercial breaks of her favorite soap opera. Now stay-at-home moms or dads buy all-natural-ingredient products with 100 percent recycled packaging recommended by an actor on an episode of *Ellen* that they probably recorded on their DVRs or streamed so they could skip the commercials. In fact, they likely didn't even watch the whole show, just a clip on some other Me's social media feed.

For decades prior to the advent of digital technology, data couldn't be disseminated broadly except on a television or radio show, and even then, you couldn't record it. To access historical information, you had to be motivated enough to go to a library and painstakingly look up something in the stacks or on micro-fiche, and even then, there was no guarantee you'd find what you were looking for. During that period, consumer-facing companies were at the height of their profitability because they controlled the product, the message, and the power. Today, my kids think the Dewey Decimal System is a band.

Then the first wave of online retail hit, which was really just a warm-up act. In Chapter 2, I talked about how many of these companies—such as Webvan and Pets.com—were ahead of their time. The *Me*tail revolution hadn't quite happened yet.

Then around 2010, internet 2.0 came along with algorithms that could generate recommendations to individual users, added to by the persuasive power of customer reviews eventually springing up everywhere and a broader consumer understanding of and experience with social media and technology. It was no longer enough to trust *Consumer Reports* magazine, which so many of us consulted before making a large purchase. Rather, it was the individual consumers' reports that became more important. It was disorienting. Pretty soon you saw stars everywhere you looked.

Over a relatively short period of time, these innovations turned millennia of history on its head. Consumers were suddenly able to become their own product, service, and experience pickers. The power had begun to shift to individuals—the Me's—and this shift marked the beginning of the *Me*tail economy.

Me, the Demographic of One

So who are these Me's?

They are all of us, from those who are young enough not to remember a time when they couldn't get anything they want from an app, to those who turn to their adult kids or grandkids for help ordering dishware from an online home goods retailer or booking a plane ticket on one of dozens of digital travel-service aggregators.

What defines them all as Me's is not that they shop at the corner store, or at the mall, or online, but that they make choices about what they want to buy based on information from sources that transcend, and upend, traditional company marketing efforts. It may be true that your company makes the best widgets or offers superb service, but it's the Me's who'll be the judge of that in the *Me*tail marketplace.

To be successful in the *Me*tail economy, businesses must never again think of consumers or their tastes and needs in terms of static demographic groups. The individual consumer now refuses to be clumped together en masse. These groups have been fractured into individual Me's who can have different needs, wants, and desires, often in the very same moment. So again, anyone hoping consistently and sustainably to serve and sell to customers must think of them in terms of an infinite number of individuals who are constantly regrouping, shifting, and changing. It's all about the individual: the Me, who is in a state of flux and able to identify with multiple tribes at once, or not at all.

For a demonstration of how this is transforming an entire sector of consumer-facing business, look no further than the media. Now, instead of a few newspapers and network television stations, Me's have access to myriad cable, newsletters, blogs, tweets, podcasts, and TikToks catering to their most esoteric interests. Substack—an online platform that provides all the infrastructure necessary for publishing content, including payment, analytics, and design infrastructure to support subscription newsletters—has enabled Me's to become their own arbiters of information, so Me's who do not recognize themselves in any of the cacophony can create even more noise of their own.

Broken Thermometer

Individualism is nothing new. Human beings have always been different things at the same time. But technology-enabled individualism has allowed us to manifest our multifaceted nature as never before.

It's not simply that Me's belong to multiple tribes. It's also that technology allows them to switch between and among them seamlessly. Imposing your expectations and narrative on consumers at a time of your choosing, which underpinned basically all marketing until present day, is as futile as trying to pick up mercury from a broken thermometer (remember those)? Instead, you should focus on helping Me's to author their own story. Or at the very least, you must try to be nimbler in helping them to move between personas.

This atomized tribalism and these complex "instaviduals" are why I think of Metail as the substantiation of quantum physics for consumers or, more specifically, as a demonstration of the principle known as quantum superposition. Like a particle in quantum physics that can be present in two places at the same time, a Me can exist simultaneously in multiple places. What these individuals may want or need in any given moment can and will change, even within the same moment.

Essentially, Me's are the "quantum consumer." Hear me out:

Quantum mechanics describes the nature of particles that make up matter—basically, how subatomic particles move and interact. Not to be confused with classical mechanics (where objects exist in a specific place at a specific time), quantum physics, or at least some quantum theory, is, well, fuzzier. It posits that these tiny specs of matter can exist simultaneously at more than one location. This subatomic system of particles is full of probabilities, as are Me's as they operate within the Metail economy.

Me's are not the same type of consumer in the space of an instant, much less a more typical marketing cycle. This is what I mean when I say we are now living through the time of a quantum consumer revolution, and this revolution has massive repercussions for any business looking to capture customers.

We've always been complex, multifaceted individuals, but this is the first time in history that an infinite number of Me's engaging in the new economy of *Me*tail has been empowered to actually have their shifting wants and needs met. Meanwhile, it is up to the company to meet them where they are, not the other way around.

Again, this is not a passing trend. It's the way the world is today, tomorrow, and at least until a newer technology supplants the internet, whereupon the awesome power of Me will be even more pronounced than before. Consumer-facing businesses haven't even begun to see the full scope of the individualism and empowerment unleashed by technology. This fact exponentially increases the complexity of serving consumers who change throughout the course of their lives, moment to moment and all at once. It's multiple persons wanting multiple things multiple ways in multiple moments. It's the individual who shops at a high-end retailer for the most expensive Balenciaga handbag, then waits 20 minutes in the buffet line in Las Vegas because she has a coupon.

So the millions of Me's out there represent millions of demographic consumers simultaneously, and the quantum consumers with millions upon millions of possibilities are giving the figurative middle finger to homogenizers of the past.

Clickbait Gone Stale

My contention, and fear, is that companies have been reacting piecemeal to this power inversion rather than responding in the full awareness of what is actually going on in the Me-centric marketplace. They think they have solved it with jargon like "omnichannel"—meaning they sell online as well as in stores—and techniques like online ads, referral bonuses, discount codes, "personalized" emails (which are anything but), tweets, texts, and social media ads. But each new thing becomes an old thing in the blink of an eye. Back when they were first introduced for example, online, banner ads had a click rate of over 20 percent but before long dropped down to 0.00002 percent.

There was a time not long ago when an effective marketing technique was to invest millions in influencers, but the Me's have already moved on from that, too. They've seen through the fact that high-priced celebrity brand ambassadors probably don't even use the product they've been hired to shill. The tribes are getting smaller as the call for authenticity from brands grows louder.

In fact, the most successful influencers today are not even trying to influence anymore. Think singer Billie Eilish and actress Zendaya, whose commitment to privacy has only served to enhance their standing with their fan base. And former boy bander Harry Styles (who you may recall graced the cover of *Vogue* magazine in a dress) sold out a $6.99 vanilla-scented candle from Target on the merest whisper on TikTok that it smelled like him. Or more precisely, his chosen scent (Tom Ford's Tobacco Vanille, which sells for $155 an ounce). Harry never mentioned the candle, or the scent he wears. Nor did he talk about a sweater he wore on a talk show that caused a viral sensation. In fact, he eschews social media unless he's promoting an album, doesn't have a TikTok account, and never uses a hashtag for anything to do with sponsorship or advertising. But it's that scarcity of posts that's making his Generation Z fans so thirsty for any sign that he liked or used a product. Harry's fans respect his elusiveness. His detachment feels more authentic and on brand somehow.

So not trying too hard to captivate your Me's, holding back a little, is working today, but tomorrow? Who knows? Harry could later face a backlash for being too aloof. The pendulum could easily swing again. The point is, when it does, Harry himself will never see it coming, because the Me's are in charge. It's not fair, but it's a fact. Whatever happens, it rests upon the whims and desires of an increasingly fickle generation of Me's, and woe betide those in the business of selling who think they've pinned them down.

Society has become so fractured, with tribes and teams splintering off into ever smaller groups, that the job of a brand marketer trying to identify different demographic groups to appeal to has become next to impossible. A great analogy is fantasy sports, which I tackle in more depth in Chapter 9. Fans now have less loyalty to a particular team because they have their own fantasy lineups, enabled, of course, by technology. Fans have "their team," which is made up of players from many different teams, as opposed to a single affiliation with an existing sports franchise. People have their own tiny group, or more likely groups, they identify with and trust the most, even if it's just a tribe of two, or one.

To be successful in the *Me*tail economy, companies are going to have to restructure their entire business model around flexibly serving the collection of Me's who matter to them most. That's the foundation of *Me*tail. That's where your focus and resources will need to be going forward, with the express goal of establishing an intimate and personal understanding of your brand's unique assortment of Me's and building new relationships with them.

What They Really, Really Want

That doesn't necessarily mean your company should try to become the next thredUP, Revolve, or Stitch Fix. There's no point in trying to duplicate whatever the app du jour happens to be, because few are making money anyway. Unicorns like DoorDash, a food delivery service, or WeWork, which simply rents out office space but was once valued like it cured cancer, have been funded through billions in venture capital to create the illusion of a successful business, but you still have to compete with them. Yes, the founders and their investors might become billionaires, even though the company may cease to exist after that transfer of wealth from pension funds to venture capitalists and on to founders. But trust me, schadenfreude will get you nowhere, and *Me*tail is here to stay.

The good news is that if you are an established brick-and-mortar company, you have an asset your digital competitors do not: physical space. That means you also have opportunities to build an intimate and lasting relationship with your Me's, gather information about them, look them in the eye, personally interact.

Online companies have discovered that they are at a disadvantage not having this physical connection. They cannot build a relationship with a customer on data algorithms alone. That's why so many online companies have been converting to "click-to-brick" operations with an ever-expanding number of physical retail locations.

Sometimes it takes an actual, face-to-face interaction with an individual customer to know what the person wants. This means that companies need associates who are well trained and paid enough to be willing to build a career with them. These salespeople will, over time, get to know their regular customers and remember details about their lives. They will play a small role in each Me's tribe. Target understood this, and you must, too. It's important now more than ever to treat frontline employees as an asset, not a cost. Too many companies treat customer service personnel, whether in a store or a call center, as a cost to be managed instead of an incredible opportunity to build a loyal Me.

In addition to the need for interaction, online companies have realized that there are certain purchases that are more likely to happen in a physical space than online. Direct-to-consumer startups with subscription services like the Dollar Shave Club are finding that, despite the hype, the profits simply aren't there—a fact I'll bet

Unilever wishes it figured out before paying a billion dollars for a company that didn't, in fact, make a single thing. It turns out that the vast majority of the population would still rather go to a brick-and-mortar store to pick up their home staples. So now Dollar Shave Club products are sold in stores just like other, more established shaving brands—hardly the paradigm-breaking model that Dollar Shave Club was once lauded to be. Yet it is not alone. Many formerly direct-to-consumer startups are now competing for shelf space in retail stores to meet Me's where they are.

Into the Gloss

Glossier is a good example of an online company that has been able to amplify its initial success by opening brick-and-mortar stores. Founded by Emily Weiss after her blog, *Into the Gloss*, went viral, the company describes itself as a "people-powered beauty ecosystem." Glossier has propelled itself past other beauty brands by cocreating products within its community of customers based on two-way conversations. In contrast to competitors who create the products first, then figure out how to sell them, Glossier puts the customer at the center of the entire process, generating loyalty among members of its tribe who feel not only that they have been heard, but that they have been authentically responded to with products made especially for them.

"The main thing Glossier stands for is the power of the individual to choose their own style, to make connections with other people, to ask questions, to understand better the things that they may want. Glossier exists purely to serve what we hear from those people about what they want," Glossier's CFO, Henry Davis, said in a recent *Forbes* magazine interview.[1]

Build It Right, and Me's Will Come

The bottom line is that brick-and-mortar is not only here to stay, but also crucial to a company's success in a *Me*tail world. The store must change, but it still needs to be a store. From now on, your company's physical space must be defined by the kind of relationship your company's Me's want to have with you. It's mission critical for you to figure out what that is.

The trick is to have time to test and zero in on the range of options that make sense for your own particular tribes—the core collection of individual Me's most likely to be drawn to what you are offering. You must be ruthlessly realistic about where you are and where you are going. Most companies are unable to do that because it can be so distressing to executives and boards to face the truth about where they stand in the consumer landscape. They would much rather pretend that their slow decline will be stopped when they install a new IT system.

If I have learned only one thing in my career, it is what I call *Joel's immutable law of transformation*: Money equals time, and time equals options. It's a simple equation. The more money you have, the more time you have. The more time you have, the more options you have. It's like $E = mc^2$ for transforming a business. Watching your company disappear or get swallowed up by a nimbler rival is one option. The other is to gather your resources and start taking time to turn things around before it's too late.

Some companies have done just that. Best Buy was headed for a ditch, but as I discuss in more detail in Chapter 6, the company rolled up its sleeves and did the hard work of shifting its narrative after ceding sales and profits to Amazon for over a decade. Amazon was killing Best Buy in the electronics space, and all the smart money thought the brick-and-mortar chain would go the way of

Blockbuster and become a footnote in retail history. But the company pivoted to the consumer and fought back as you'll read later.

In the *Me*tail economy, it takes unrelenting attention to your customer to remain on the leading edge.

*Me*tail Strategies for Your Company's Future

In the following chapters, I am going to lay out for you multiple models for attracting Me's in the *Me*tail era, so that you can see how each one applies to your own business, or not. Again, you need to take honest stock of what you have, what differentiates you from the competition, and what your customer values in you most. Have detailed conversations with the individuals who walk into your stores or buy from you online to discover exactly how you can enhance their experience, giving them what they want and need, and then deliver it in a way that makes the most sense for you and them. Cultivate an authentic relationship with your customer and engage in some meaningful dialogue. Listen, learn, and then align your investment and resources accordingly.

Why? Because there is no going back. Access and information have completely shifted the balance of power in favor of the consumer. Companies are just a part of the selling process, not the selling process itself. They are not the end, but the means—a mere part of the narrative as the Me's create their own consumer journeys. Accept this fact and base all your decision-making upon this new reality. Once you fully embrace the *Me*tail economy, those hungry internet giants gobbling up consumer dollars will no longer seem like such a threat. Indeed, once you acknowledge their power, the Me's will help you in your long-overdue reinvention. You may even find yourself doing something that doesn't make money in the moment in order to make money in the future by capturing the loyalty of your customer in a *Me*tail world. Trust that instinct, because it means you are on the right path.

Again, as long as human beings walk this earth, there will be consumers. The difference today is that they are now the most important part of the equation. They sit at the tippy top of that transactional pyramid. It's just a question of reorienting your company around the needs and desires of your particular set of Me's.

Onward.

ME

PART II

SIX INGREDIENTS FOR *ME*TAIL SUCCESS

Over these next pages, I am going to give you stories about each *Me*tail ingredient so that you can see yourself, or pieces of yourself, or not at all in the experiences of other companies. At a minimum, you will gain some clarity about what you are, or are not, to your consumer in this newfound self-awareness.

Meanwhile, I want you to approach the six Cs—my six models for competing in a *Me*tail world—more as a set of essential cooking ingredients. There is no perfect recipe. The six Cs—cost, convenience, category expert, customization, curation, and community—are simply the time-tested attributes that can create a bond between a company and the consumer. The Cs are a distillation of those elements that define the nature of the relationship and a way to orient yourself as you reimagine your *Me*tail strategy. Running a profitable consumer-oriented business is about having a relationship with your customers, your Me's; and the six Cs are the building blocks for a visceral and lasting connection. Keep it simple and leverage the ingredients to cook the tastiest dish for your own set of Me's.

So think of Part II of this book as you might a cooking lesson. I am not giving you the recipe, just the "mystery basket" of ingredients from which to build your own dish. Some you may discard entirely. Others you might use more or less of, as you season your particular dish. But do not search here for the step-by-step instructions, measurements, or timing. Your recipe is your own. You will tweak it to make it work for you and your Me's. The ingredients are what matters. How you use them is up to you.

4

COST:
GIVE ME A STEAL

Price is what you pay, value is what you get.

—WARREN BUFFETT

Let's face it—everyone loves a bargain.

Most of us can quickly conjure up an idea of what the *cost model* looks like and understand its attraction to so many businesses. Apples to apples, who doesn't want to pay less than someone else? But for a long time, cost was difficult to objectively determine. It was more about how someone felt about the price-value exchange versus the dead-net-lowest cost. However, in the *Me*tail era, price information is at every Me's fingertips, and while bargains on goods and services will inevitably find buyers, competing at the lowest cost has become much more challenging. Even those of means think twice about paying full retail, and shopping at retailers across the cost spectrum has become almost chic. You now have countless Me's shopping in a cost-conscious way who wouldn't have been caught dead in an off-price retailer even 10 years ago.

Of course, some need a bargain more than others, particularly post-COVID, where millions of families have had to learn how to stretch a dollar. More Me's seek out the cheapest option in a recession or crisis, amid widespread job layoffs and furloughs, because they simply must. But that behavior carries forward. There are Me's who like a steal for other reasons. These Me's might believe in spending more on items like shoes or handbags, for example, eager to be seen with the right "it" bag on their arm no matter what the price, and yet they still stock up on a 10-pack of tube socks. Whatever drives your Me's to hunt for the best deal, know that there is more to becoming a successful cost *Me*tailer than you might think.

That's because definitions matter. Cost means cost, not value. Value is too ephemeral to make it a C. Do shoppers care about value? Sure, sometimes—maybe even often. But value is relative, and cost is absolute. So as you read this chapter, resist the temptation to confuse the two. Prior to *Me*tail, many retailers could compete on cost whether they were lowest cost or not, because the information advantage—the power—rested with the company. Today, if you want to be cost competitive, you must mean it and understand the implications that has on the way you must orient your cost structure as well as your strategy.

Value Exchange

Too many companies have found themselves contemplating the cost model of *Me*tail at one time or another. When little if anything you are offering is differentiated, the main way to compete is to provide products at a low enough cost to attract customers. Cost-model competitors like Dollar General and Walmart modeled their entire businesses around low cost and grew economic profit through sheer scale. That can still be a winning formula.

But if that's your strategy, then you must root out costs wherever you can to pass those savings along to the consumer. Too many former cost competitors have allowed costs to creep into their businesses, making it more difficult to retain the title of lowest cost. With information available to everyone, either you are the lowest cost or you are not—hard stop. That's why this C exclusively is not for most of you.

To use just one example, it's a common misperception that Costco is a cost player; based on its name, that's understandable. But it certainly doesn't offer the cheapest goods in town. Rather, it offers a narrow selection of quality products in large quantities, or sharply-priced individual items, all at relatively competitive prices on a per-unit basis. So if you're buying food for a Thanksgiving gathering of 30 extended family members, you're in good shape. But if you only want a package of muffins sized for a family of four, you might be better off going to your local supermarket. The point is that Costco customers value cost (among other Cs), but they do not view Costco as the absolute lowest cost for most items, unless they are buying in bulk. You might say that Costco has chosen a pinch of the cost ingredient, but just a pinch.

Cost-focused Me's want to know that whatever they are buying—whether that's a single bottle of Windex at a dollar store or a pair of $8 jeans from Primark or a tankful of the cheapest gas for their car—they are paying (and can check that it is) the absolute lowest cost. The competitive strategy here is simply that you're offering the best deal possible.

Another Me's Treasure

Like Costco, most companies will probably not gravitate toward the 100 percent cost C, because even Me's interested in lowest cost have raised their expectations. Could you? Sure, and if so, go ahead and skip to Chapter 10. But if you imagine that cost will be just one ingredient in your complex recipe, let me illustrate why other ingredients are necessary.

The cost model was much more basic when I was growing up in suburban Massachusetts. My family was an early adopter of off-price, and our secret weapon was a chaotic and cavernous discount store called Building #19½.

The place was an old, disused warehouse in Burlington on the northwestern outskirts of Boston. It sold everything from carpets to household cleaners and children's underwear in random piles and racks on the shop floor. Literally anything you could think of except for fresh groceries could be found in a bargain bin if you were persistent enough, even "genuine prison sneakers." One of the handmade signs hanging from the 40-foot ceiling read, "Helpful Shopping Tip #19 IF YOU CAN'T FIND WHAT YOU'RE LOOKING FOR, YOU SHOULD PROBABLY JUST BUY SOMETHING ELSE."

Mom would write up a list of stuff we needed, make sure we synchronized our watches (this was long before the days of cell phones), and instruct us to meet her back at the cash registers in an hour. It was like going on a scavenger hunt . . . if mismatched but "close-enough" socks and bottles of off-brand bleach could be considered treasures.

One of the first stores in the nation to sell closeout consumer goods at rock-bottom prices, the original Building #19 opened in 1964 in the Bethlehem Hingham Shipyard, where the buildings were all numbered. One of the store's two cofounders, Harry

Andler, had been doing a surplus and salvage business in the ship-yard for years, seeking out and buying up whatever he could get a good deal on. The story goes that when he opened the store with his partner, Jerry Ellis, an outsized personality with a flair for marketing, the two kept the store name because they were too cheap to change the sign. It became such a running gag that whenever they opened a new location, they added a fraction to the original name: Building #19½, Building #19¾, and so forth (there were 13 locations at the chain's peak).

To call it cluttered would be a gross understatement. The place looked as if it had just been looted; actually, it was so messy even looters would not loot it, but what did it matter at those prices? (Turns out, in a *Me*tail world, it actually *does* matter, but more on this later.) One of the Massachusetts closeout chain's entrance signs had a self-caricature of Jerry with the words "Home of the Good Stuff Cheap, Come on In, and Bring MONEY!" As shoppers walked in, they were invited to try the free coffee with "fake cream" on a coffee stand emblazoned with another gag: "Don't make fun of our coffee. Someday you'll be old and weak yourself."

The messages were engagingly humble, referencing the fact that the place was a mess and everything was cheap. "Chateau de Cheapo" champagne was the reward if customers could find a better price elsewhere.

This groan-worthy humor wasn't limited to signs like the one with a pig saying, "I never sausage a place," or an Oscar the Grouch look-alike (there was no way the owners paid Sesame Street Workshop for a real endorsement) saying, "This is my kinda place . . . A real dump!" Even 19's weekly fliers looked like comic strips, usually featuring another cartoon figure of Jerry making a bad pun like "Lighten Up! Without Lightening Your Wallet" for that moment's deal on mini lanterns, or "Great Sound at Prices That Are Music to Your Ears" for headphones.

Not that it has anything to do with *Me*tail or the Cs, but I can't resist sharing a few of their other Borscht Belt humor slogans:

Suffer a little, save a lot

Please leave with as many children as you came with

America's messiest department store

Free ride in a police car if you shoplift

Prices that won't scare the pooh out of you (featuring a caterpillar reading a *Winnie the Pooh* book—again, likely in copyright violation—in the book department)

You get the idea.

But the real genius of the place was how Harry scavenged the globe for deals he could pass on to the consumer. Before any other merchandiser thought to do so at scale, he found discontinued items, products near their expiration date, factory irregulars, fire sales, and customs' seizures. It didn't matter what the items were. They could have been perfectly functioning white goods with slight imperfections like scratches and dents, or discontinued girls' blouses in unfortunate shades of mustard. Harry even followed bankruptcy filings to learn which companies might need access to quick cash.

But all good things must come to an end, and in 2013, the Building #19 chain itself filed for bankruptcy. Jerry blamed the internet, more manufacturing overseas, and especially (though likely tongue in cheek) the improved fire protection of warehouses. But the way I see it, the biggest reason for the reduced customer traffic was sector competition. Other discount stores figured out the formula and made it better. With so many discount chains and dollar stores springing up across the country, Building #19 needed to do more than wrap bad puns around their bargain basement prices. As much as I enjoyed the self-effacing humor, it wasn't a sustainable business model.

Perfect Circle

But the model was not dead; the recipe just needed another ingredient or two. Take Ollie's Bargain Outlet, for example, which opened its first store in Harrisburg, Pennsylvania, in 1982. Like Building #19's goal back in the day, Ollie's goal is to find the best closeout deals and pass the savings along to its customers. Its buyers also comb the world for overstocked items, manufacturer-refurbished goods, products with irregularities, closeouts, and packaging changes.

And just as it was for Building #19, Ollie's inventory is never the same store to store, retaining that "treasure hunt" feel because you never know what you're going to get.

But somehow, Ollie's managed to quietly become one of the country's largest closeout chains, with almost 400 stores and counting. Why? Because Ollie's recognized the changing consumer and understood that Me's were simply not going to dig through disorganized piles of stuff, no matter how much they might save. Walk into any Ollie's, and you might not even realize that you are in a closeout store at all. The shelves are neat (mostly), and the store is merchandised into categories, so it is easier to find what you are looking for. It's that simple: Building #19 but with a better shopping experience (convenience).

Again, Ollie's is much more organized than most of its hard-discount competitors and almost as well organized as some under-performing general-merchandise retailers. Shopping in Ollie's stores is significantly less exhausting than shopping in its many competitors. All those bargains are possible to find without losing an entire afternoon. It also allows for buyer's remorse, with a 30-day "No Hard Time" guarantee, which is rare for closeout retailers.

Ollie's particular cost model formula has proved so successful, especially during the COVID-induced recession, that it's been rolling out dozens of new stores across the country. Each new outlet opening is a major event, with jammed parking lots, armed guards at the door to wrangle the crowds, and people lining up around the block waiting to get in. It also does no business online—another example of deciding to compete where it can and not trying to be all things to all people. Ollie's is not the only deep discounter out there, but it is by far the most successful, running laps around its competitors.

In a perfect-circle moment, Ollie's recently took over the lease for the original Building #19 in Massachusetts. In an homage to the granddaddy of discount chains, Ollie's is calling the location "Ollie's @ Building 19."

As Jerry Altland, an executive at Ollie's, explained to the locals assembled at the new store opening, "Our stores are very similar to Building #19, but a helluva lot cleaner."[1]

The fate of Building #19 and its stack-it-high-and-let-it-fly competition proves my point that the cost model in its purest form probably isn't enough to make it in *Me*tail anymore—at least not at scale. Ollie's does sell the good stuff cheap, but it's an environment that's more appealing to customers, with a pinch of convenience here and a dash of curation there. Ollie's has found a way to compete inside the cost model but with an understanding of the other Cs and how to use them in just the right amount to bake a better cake.

The Greenbacks

Of course, Ollie's isn't the only cost-model business that's been thriving in the best and worst of times. Dollar stores, in particular Dollar General and Dollar Tree, have been proliferating across the country to the point where, in the United States, 75 percent of the population lives within five miles of one.[2] And the concept is blossoming worldwide as well. They are banking on the fact that consumers would rather take a two-minute ride (or more likely walk) to pick up a gallon of milk and a small box of garbage bags versus 15 to 20 minutes, plus the negotiation of vast stores and parking lots, to get it done at a superstore.

These stores did particularly well during the pandemic because they pivoted quickly to provide the staples that appeal to consumers who've become not only more cost conscious but also concerned with convenience and safety, including and especially the switch to food and cleaning supplies. At the time of writing, there were more than 31,000 locations for this type of retailer across the United States alone. To put that in perspective, there are more dollar stores in the United States than there are McDonald's restaurants. Dollar General dominates with a network of 17,000 stores and is continually adding to its physical footprint. The chain's small-box store format was designed specifically for quick access to a broad assortment of everyday essentials.

Originally located in "food deserts"—rural areas with populations of 20,000 or less and underserved city neighborhoods— these dollar store chains realized that there was also a place for them in the suburbs, where middle-class families appreciate the ease of access as well as the fact that these stores have what they need at a lower cost.

And even in the post-pandemic wage inflation environment, the future of the dollar store is bright.

Because consumers of all income levels have become increasingly cost conscious, there has been a steady year-on-year growth of Dollar General, which has had positive comparable sales for 30 years. As a result, its share price grew sixfold over the past decade. (Dollar Tree's shares quadrupled over the same time period.)

Dollar stores, also known as "greenback stores," have shown themselves to be remarkably resilient during economic downturns.

And not just because their Me's were being squeezed. The dollar stores' customers appreciated the fact that their supply chain was reliable. They stayed open through the COVID-19 crisis, reassuringly and consistently supplying all the basics, especially the fresh, cooler-stored food at Dollar General. That dependability has resonated among the chain's customers, whatever their socioeconomic backgrounds.

Unlimited Possibilities

It would be too easy to dismiss the dollar store cost model by saying, "We can't sell our product at a dollar." And that's how most saw it. Until one didn't. Five Below took the ingredient and (you guessed it) changed the recipe. In 2002, Five Below saw the incredible penetration that dollar stores were having throughout the United States and thought, "Here's an *idea*. What if instead of $1, we sold things for $5 or less?" It was a *big idea* since now, all of a sudden, these stores could stock a much bigger and more appealing assortment of merchandise. It was a *genius idea* because it opened up a huge range of possibilities for the company's customers (and the company itself) with this category, attracting a bigger, broader range of Me's as a result. It has since grown to more than 1,000 stores in 38 states.

A *Washington Post* article on the chain accurately described it as "a wonderland of things no one needs."[3] The stores, which are located mostly in strip malls, invite shoppers to "let go and have fun." Five Below's buyers pay close attention to what's not only cheap, but trending. Far from being focused on the nondiscretionary, its website banner reads "amazing experience with unlimited possibilities." The stores are organized into eight Five Below Worlds: Style, Room, Sports, Tech, Create, Party, Candy, and

Now (which presumably means whatever silly object is trending on TikTok).

Five Below is kind of like an entire store's worth of impulse-buy items you might find at the checkout of a typical big-box retailer, but cheaper and more indulgent. Mini Bluetooth speakers that light up all colors of the rainbow, cutesy makeup pouches for tween girls, retro whoopee cushions, and Aqua Splash water guns are the kinds of "must-have" novelties you might discover as you negotiate the aisles. The low prices make these small splurges easier to justify, although consumers are often surprised by how much their shopping baskets add up to by the time they reach the checkout counter.

But it is not all fun and games. A $5 threshold allows Five Below to also stock necessities like household items, as well as fitness equipment, home decor, back-to-school supplies, and technology items at discount prices, and a few splurges at $6 to $10, just as (spoiler alert) dollar stores all carry items for more than a dollar.

There was some concern that because Five Below's mix skewed a bit more toward frivolity, its merchandise wouldn't fly off the shelves at quite the same speed during the pandemic. Oh, but it did, once the lockdowns ended. Based on the retailer's stellar financial performance, consumers stuck mostly at home were seeking affordable opportunities for fun more than ever. The numbers suggest it's doing something right with its hybrid of affordability and tween-whispering merchandising.

It's indicative of the elasticity of the cost model that Five Below expanded its retail concept to include Five Beyond, allowing the retailer to exploit a pricing loophole in its marketplace messaging to offer an even broader range of products. In 2020, the company added permanent Five Beyond sections in 140 of its Five Below stores and announced plans to introduce this store-within-a-store concept into 30 percent of its locations by the end of 2021. Five

Below also has a seasonal "Wow Wall" with pricier items at some of its locations.

Five Below and Ollie's both prove what can be done if you get creative with the cost C. Too many would have thought if you were to take the cost model to its logical conclusion, there would have to be nickel stores, but Ollie's and Five Below went the other way and won.

Designer Deals

In fact, there is a broad spectrum of cost-conscious Me's and numerous ways to package deals, whether that's curating frivolity and fun, making it extremely convenient to pick up the essentials, or giving someone a bargain-hunting fix at an outlet store like TJ Maxx, Marshall's, Saks Off Fifth, Kohl's, Ross, and Nordstrom Rack. These companies have outperformed in recent years for the same reason suburban moms might pick up soda and bread at Dollar General or hop on a Southwest flight to Albuquerque: because low cost is hard to resist, no matter your income bracket. These off-price retailers have garnered a large and growing following just as the larger, full-price chains are struggling and closing stores.

It's one reason why Nordstrom has invested more into Nordstrom Rack than its traditional store formats of late and anticipates that its Rack business will make up about half of total revenues in the near future, compared with about a third as I write this.

Nordstrom Rack offers a slightly different value proposition from its off-price peers, once again proving my point that there is a lot of range within this particular C to differentiate yourself. Whereas TJ Maxx offers a limited amount of higher-end name-brand items (such as Vince and Tory Burch in its "Runway" section), its locations tend to be more what you would expect from a discount store: a little jumbled and random.

Nordstrom understood that cost was important to some Me's who might not otherwise be able to or might not want to shop the brand in its full-price locations. As it saw Me's gravitating toward this model, Nordstrom added a pinch more cost into its recipe, then a pinch more, and so on.

My point is that there's room for all iterations and price points of these discount stores, which have been steadily taking market share. But what these off-pricers must never forget is that they exist to offer their Me's the lowest prices possible, which is why the move of some off-pricers to sell online puzzles me. They risk veering away from their core competitive strength by adding to their operational complexity and expense. It's not clear that they have figured out which C they are adding to their recipe. While Nordstrom Rack retails at price points that can support online sales and can plug into the operational ecosystem of Nordstrom for online orders, I have to wonder if any of the lower-tier brick-and-mortar off-price players can pull it off—without degrading profitability too significantly over time but perhaps they are listening to a consumer I can't hear, in which case, bravo.

By contrast, the e-commerce startup Italic has figured out a way to bring discounted premium goods to its Me's by eliminating one thing that drives cost in branded products: the brand itself. It buys directly from the factories that make high-end designer apparel and accessories for brands such as Prada, Givenchy, Armani, Burberry, and Vilebrequin, partnering with them to manufacture the same quality items under the Italic label. Italic, which has the tagline "Quality, at Cost," can afford to sell direct to the consumer at cost because its business model is subscription-based. So if you sign on for the $120-a-year subscription, a cashmere hoodie that would normally sell under a designer label at a luxury department store for $500, or at an off-price retailer for $300, can be bought for $65.

Italic isn't the only direct-to-consumer retailer to offer luxury goods this way. M. Gemi does it for Italian artisan-made leather shoes, for example. But Italic has found a way to be an online "cost" model player in the off-price market with a well-curated array of product categories from jewelry to houseware, bedding, and luxury candles at, like-for-like, far lower prices than its designer-brand counterparts. The most expensive item on the Italic website at the time of this writing, for example, is a $220 tote from the same factory that makes Prada handbags that sell for more than $3,000.

"I had always thought it backwards that manufacturers take home the smallest margin in the supply chain despite making the actual products being sold for many times the cost," explained founder Jeremy Cai. "Italic bridges the gap between consumers and luxury goods by partnering directly with the manufacturers instead of purchasing inventory like a brand."[4]

Just because these items are sold at a fraction of the cost, without the designer label slapped on the back, doesn't make them any less desirable to today's savvy Me's.

At the time of writing, Italic announced they were moving away from the subscription model. I'll be interested to see how that impacts their Me's.

The diversity of examples illustrated above and their breadth of price points prove that whatever service or product your business is selling, there is a vast range of possibility within the cost model, just as the Me's you are transacting with are infinite in their variety and motives. Your prices will get them in the door, but they'll keep coming back for a host of other reasons as their needs and desires evolve. That's why it behooves any cost-model *Me*tailer to never, ever look upon its Me's as cheap, no matter what their income levels may be in a given moment.

Valued Customers

Cricket Wireless understood the potential of cost- and value-conscious Me's when it began expanding beyond its Chicago footprint, where it was serving a more credit-challenged customer base. It launched in 2009 under its initial owner, Leap Wireless, to give underserved communities access to a mobile phone service via a prepaid service, where customers could pay on their debit cards or refill their data-usage balances at a Cricket store, often in cash. It sold packages costing anywhere from $30 to $70 a month according to usage, as well as a range of cheap but serviceable cell phones.

But just because the costs of products and bundled packages were kept low, this didn't mean that customers were treated poorly. Cricket made a point of treating this core group of Me's with respect.

"For a lot of our customers, this is the only connection they have to the internet," explained Cricket president John Dwyer soon after he took the helm in 2016. "A lot of our customers don't have home broadband and don't have pay TV services at home. As a result, they'll buy a smartphone, they'll hold onto it and they'll use it for all their access to the world. So, we want to make sure for this price-sensitive segment, that they really understand the value that they're getting and that they feel good about it—they feel respected and well taken care of."[5]

That, in a nutshell, is how every cost-model company should view its consumers: with respect. Cricket has since become a national carrier with more than 16 million users.

Blue-Sky Savings

Southwest Airlines does as much for its passengers. One of the earliest and largest of the low-cost airlines, it modeled itself after Pacific Southwest, which launched in California as an interstate carrier in 1949. By not flying over state lines, PSA managed to avoid federal regulation and the expenses that went with it. Seeing what PSA was doing and the way it was making air travel more affordable to middle-class consumers, Southwest did the same thing in Texas when it launched in 1971. But blue skies opened up for Southwest after deregulation of the industry in 1978, and the upstart carrier became more intentional in its low-cost strategy.

While its more established competitors like Pan Am, TWA, and United were providing white-glove service, with real silver, glass, and chinaware for their jet-setting class of Me's, Southwest developed a low-cost strategy, cutting out all the extras to enable more price-conscious customers (who might otherwise drive or hop on a Greyhound bus) to fly. It stuck to a single type of aircraft for its fleet, making it more efficient to train pilots and mechanics and limiting the types of spare parts it needed to maintain its aircraft. It scheduled flights to enable shorter turnarounds for increased aircraft utilization and focused on popular but shorter routes for higher passenger volume. It chose to go only through smaller airports, lowering landing fees.

Southwest was focused and creative in the way it oriented its business model around cost efficiencies so that it could pass the savings onto its consumers. But Southwest was never cheap. The company didn't scrimp on how it treated its employees, paying them well and providing profit sharing. Southwest realized that flight crews were more likely to treat their passengers well if they themselves felt respected and invested in the success of the company. So the only thing about the airline that felt cheap was the price of the ticket.

Where Southwest does invest is in its hiring. It screens potential employees to make sure they're the right fit for its brand: friendly and approachable. Its recruitment practices never deviate from this standard. Attitude is everything for a consumer-facing business that prides itself on being people-oriented—a lesson that any company should take to heart in a *Me*tail economy, whatever C that company chooses.

During the pandemic, Southwest also gave its passengers policies far more flexible than any other airline, allowing them to cancel 30 minutes ahead of the flight and putting the cost of the ticket toward their next journey. In other words, Southwest's leaders put themselves in the shoes of their customers and did what was right.

More recently, as other airlines caught onto their strategy, Southwest has found further opportunities to retain its cost advantage, including putting lighter-weight seats in its cabins and winglets on its aircraft wing tips for greater fuel efficiency. It also carefully invested in larger aircraft with greater capacity and retired older planes, further enhancing fuel efficiency while increasing passenger loads.

That's the thing about being a cost player: The cost-saving formula can never be static, as the search for operational efficiencies must continue throughout the lifetime of the business. Of course, you cannot stop investing in your company, but you must invest only in the things connected to your C model. Southwest has been relentless in finding new ways to safely cut costs, never relying on one area for savings and always seeking new opportunities as technologies advance. The airline's forward thinking and innovative logistics solutions have enabled it to continue beating other carriers on cost, despite ongoing industry disruptions.

Race to the Bottom

The Southwest model was so successful that it has since been emulated around the world, with varying degrees of success. The British carrier EasyJet and the Dublin-based airline Ryanair are two examples of cost-model carriers that took Southwest's template for trimming costs almost to the point of the absurd.

Ryanair, which launched in 1984 to compete with British Airway's Dublin-to-London route, switched to the Southwest model in the early 1990s, trimming its costs to the point where its aircraft seating resembles something you might see on a public bus in a former Eastern Bloc nation: hard and narrow with color accents in the shade of, as one travel blogger put it, "puke yellow."[6]

Ryanair also saves on costs by operating mostly between second-tier airports. At the time of writing, it flew to 36 countries and 215 cities year-round and seasonally, growing steadily based on passengers who can't resist a $25 round-trip ticket for a Mediterranean holiday in Split, Croatia. They have their eyes wide open about any extra charges if they want the luxury of, say, not being relegated to a middle seat in the back row next to the bathroom; or bringing a carry-on bag slightly larger than a shoebox; or boarding first; or checking in at the airport as opposed to checking in online and printing out their boarding passes at home.

Ryanair's travelers know what to expect, and the bare-knuckle experience of checking in, boarding, flying, and deplaning is almost a badge of honor for some passengers, who can't wait to boast to their friends about how cheap their weekend in Corfu was. For the most part, these Me's cheerfully permit themselves to be herded onto the aircraft like cattle, even if that means standing on the tarmac for 20 minutes in the rain waiting to board because most of Ryanair's airport destinations don't have jetways. Somehow, this group of Me's seems to be in on the joke.

EasyJet, which launched in 1996 with flights to Glasgow, Edinburgh, and Amsterdam, doesn't go quite that far, although it does charge punitive fees for such airport services as in-person check-ins because it's trying to lower the number of airport staff to keep costs down. The price of checking a bag can be higher than the ticket itself. And don't expect to have somewhere to sit as you wait at your gate to board. You'll have to queue with the rest of the herd.

Most travel reviewers cannot say which of these European airlines, along with Jet2 and the unfortunately named Wizz airlines, is best, or worst. There are so many variables, from routing and flight schedules, which are so specific to each of these carriers, to a Me's ability to physically endure a hard seat for three to six hours.

What is happening with these cost carriers is more than just providing cheap seats and subsequent higher plane loads. They are not necessarily making their passengers feel special with friendly customer service. Instead, they're offering a vast array of choices to appeal to the vast array of Me's. Their customers like the unbundled approach because it puts the power completely in their hands. Me's can decide what is important to them and how much they're willing to pay for a flight with a side of leg room.

The "cheap-seat" Me's do the math. They measure the carry-on allowance and buy luggage specifically approved for the airline they are choosing.

Cost Optimizer

In some respects, Southwest is to the airline industry what Walmart is to retail, with its scrupulous emphasis on cost control. And of course, no chapter on cost would be complete without mentioning the world's largest retailer and the archetypal cost-model company.

The big-box retail pioneer, Walmart, initially focused on rural America where there was a dearth of retail and the costs of labor and real estate were lowest. It was the first to source most of its goods from overseas factories, where labor costs were lowest; it warehoused its merchandise in proximity to its stores to reduce transportation expenses and quickly stock its shelves; and it generally went much further than any other company in cutting costs to pass along to its customers.

There is even rumored to be a time when the Bentonville, Arkansas–based retail behemoth made its executives share hotel rooms when they traveled. The company had set up every piece of the business to be a low-cost provider. Its whole existence was based on having good enough products at prices better than everyone else's.

Walmart optimizes the cost model by using its massive size—with stores in 27 countries serving 100 million customers a week to negotiate the best deals with its suppliers. Despite competition from Amazon and the emergence of dollar stores and other deep-discount stores, Walmart is often the only major brick-and-mortar store in a given town providing a wide range of food, clothing, and household goods at low prices, and that presence in and of itself creates a vast and dependable customer base. In fact, 90 percent of Americans live within 10 miles of a Walmart.

Walmart did a slight rebrand in 2008, changing its slogan from "Always low prices. Always" to "Save money. Live better," with advertising showing its Me's enjoying the money they just saved by shopping at Walmart and showing how all those incremental price cuts add up. The campaign built off an economic study by Global Insight claiming Walmart's lower prices saved US shoppers $2,500 per household in 2006, or $957 per person. Walmart also built an interactive website named for the new slogan that encouraged visitors to leave testimonials about how much they saved, which of course quickly added up to hundreds of millions of dollars.

It was a subtle shift. The retailer was basically saying that it's not so much the price of each individual item as the totality of savings when you do most of your discretionary and nondiscretionary spending in a Walmart store. The result is greater choice for Me's in terms of where else their income goes. It was Walmart's way of beginning to give their customers control of the narrative, and it worked. The company got its cost model exactly right.

This success makes it all the more puzzling that Walmart is currently throwing resources in the opposite direction. Lately, you could be forgiven for not knowing precisely what Walmart stands for. It introduced its own program to compete with Amazon Prime, spent billions buying unprofitable direct-to-consumer internet companies, and even launched a service called Jetblack, a high-end private concierge service in New York City, along with other expensive forays in the opposite direction of cost.

Jetblack, the subscription program, which cost $50 a month, used artificial intelligence to recommend products to wealthier customers in Manhattan and Brooklyn and enabled users to text orders for nonperishable items to Jetblack to receive delivery right at their doorsteps, even products from other local retailers and suppliers. An intriguing way to think about competing in a *Me*tail economy, to be sure. But how could a true cost player imagine this would make sense to its Me's? It was such a flop that it reportedly cost Walmart $15,000 a year for each Jetblack subscriber,[7] leaving analysts scratching their heads about what the retail giant executives were thinking. Executives are, of course, spinning it as an important learning experience, but that's a pretty common refrain in situations like this.

By February 2020, Walmart course-corrected, discontinuing Jetblack and scaling down the e-commerce acquisitions that never fit its core cost model, like ModCloth and Bonobos. It also closed its Hayneedle's Omaha headquarters, getting back to its cost-conscious roots so that its Me's can benefit. And just when its Me's needed their superstores most, Walmart weathered the COVID crisis remarkably well, achieving all-time sales highs as it maintained its supply chains and offered all the competitively priced essentials its locked-down Me's could have asked for. None of which required an AI-driven concierge.

While in my view the dot-com acquisitions (Moosejaw, Vudu, Art.com, Eloquii, Bonobos, etc.) and the launch of Jetblack were mistakes, it remains to be seen how this overall strategy of investing in offerings beyond Walmart's core cost model will play out. But it is instructive that the retail giant is currently in the process of shutting down many of these companies and services and, as executives from the acquired companies leave, folding what's left into its existing operations. It's likely that Walmart executives significantly underestimated the costs of trying to compete with Amazon. Perhaps they needed to spend $3.3 billion on an over-hyped Amazon competitor called Jet.com, for the technology (though I doubt it). Even so, they would have had to understand that the $3.3 billion was just the tip of the iceberg. Maybe they would have made the same choices; maybe not.

This unwinding of what was surely a conscious strategy shift brings us back to the importance of focusing, knowing your recipe, and understanding what it will take to change course.

Beware of the potential hazards of trying to be something you are not, but please do not take the wrong lessons away. There is nothing wrong with pursuing different strategies, but they must be fully thought through from a customer lens. You need to ask not only "Would a customer like this?" but "Would *our* customer like this?" Then take the time to understand the full cost (money, time, people) it will take to provide it.

If your chosen model is cost, you need to orient your all your operations around being able to make money at the lowest possible price. Walmart drifted, but it probably righted its ship in time. It could afford to drift, but many companies cannot.

This is not to suggest you should put your cheapest foot forward or approach the cost model like some local used-car dealer or Crazy Eddie, who shouted on the cheesy TV ads, "I'm offering you prices so low, I'm gonna get fired!" (though he probably would have preferred that to jail, where he ended up for a time for a fraud conviction). Market yourself that way if you must, but never forget that your Me's are smart shoppers. If you are not truly offering them the best deal, they'll soon find out about it. Me's have access to price information as never before.

Don't assume a price-matching guarantee will make up for it. Making your customer do all the work by finding evidence of a lower price elsewhere is off-putting.

Again, never underestimate your price-savvy Me's. Deliver on your cost promise or risk losing their loyalty the moment they do the math.

Items in Your Cart

The cost model is about cost, not value. Cost can mean many things to many Me's. But at the end of the day, you must be the lowest cost. Not necessarily *only* the lowest cost—you can be other things too—but you must be the lowest cost. There is no room for ambiguity on this point.

However, the cost model probably isn't enough to make it on its own in *Me*tail. It's too easy for someone else to come along and undercut you. You need to create an appealing environment with other Cs, but with intention and focus, always asking, "How does this attribute relate to my desire to be the lowest-cost player?"

Every price point and every category has room for lowest-cost players. Identify the range of products where you want to compete and then stick to it, but lowest cost doesn't relegate you to only the cheapest product categories.

Never look on your Me's as cheap, no matter their income level. Your prices will get them in the door, but they'll keep coming back because you respect them.

Operationally, your cost-saving formula should never be static. The search for operational efficiencies must continue throughout the lifetime of the business. Investments must be made, but through a lens of "How does this keep me the lowest-cost player?"

Unbundle. Give your Me's a choice about what they pay for by giving it to them on an à la carte menu, like the European discount airlines. Many Me's like the unbundled approach because it puts the power in their hands. They can decide what is important to them and how much they're willing to spend.

Choose your C and stick to it. If it's cost, then be at the best possible price vis-à-vis all your competitors who are offering the same products. Orient your entire operations around being able to make money at the lowest-possible price. Find ways to distinguish yourself from your competition within this category, but never forget your roots as a cost player. Or find another C.

Your cart total: *Cost!*

Proceed to next chapter . . .

5

CONVENIENCE: MAKE IT EASY FOR ME

Ease your customer's pain.

—HAZEL EDWARDS, OWNER OF GILLIAN ROBERTS BRIDAL GOWNS

I love getting gas at Costco, and not only because it's the cheapest gas around. It's because Costco makes its gas hoses extra long. So if I happen to pull up to the pump on the opposite side of the car my gas tank is on, I don't have the anxiety of having to turn the vehicle around in a tight space with other cars lined up right behind me waiting their turn. Instead, I can just pull the extra-long hose around my car—something I cannot do anywhere else, because the standard gas station hose is only about six feet long. It also means all the other drivers who arrive on the wrong side won't slow me down, and we can all get our gas sooner.

It's a small but meaningful thing that Costco has thought of and built into its design that makes its customers' lives easier. Same goes for the wider parking spaces Costco paints to reduce parking anxiety. Most consumers see it the same way: an added convenience they appreciate. But don't assume this is something purely altruistic that Costco is doing. In the case of the gas pump hoses, it means many more cars per hour can drive through and fill up on gas. The line at the pump is virtually unbroken all day long, which in turns helps Costco make up through volume for the lower gas prices it charges. Its pump design is the perfect example of linking the *convenience model* to a business benefit.

Convenience seems simple enough: Make it easy for Me. Stand out among your competition by enabling time-pressed, harried consumers to come in and out of your store location or e-commerce site as stress free as possible, with goods that are merchandised in ways that can be easily discovered and added to their shopping carts. To do this, a company must always put itself in the shoes of its Me's and think of all the little things that make the transaction smooth. The thing is, many companies say this is one of their Cs, but very few companies truly think that way.

How many times have you found an item and your size was missing? Or the item you came for was out of stock after you spent 20 minutes trying to find a parking space before even entering the store? Or when you went to check out, only 2 out of 10 registers were open?

Or did you have to hunt for some necessity because it was stuck in the back of the store? Those companies are making the whole experience about *their* needs, and not what is best for their Me's. It's the same reason for cluttered supermarket aisles, which are common in bigger cities like New York where rents are high and companies want to sell as much per square foot as possible. Store managers often place promotional displays in the already crowded aisles in the hope of encouraging more impulse buys. But that move makes it harder for their customers to find or access what they came in for in the first place. When consumers experience these obstacles too many times, or even once, they vote with their feet, or fingers, clicking their orders on Amazon.

Convenience is in the eye of the customer, *not* the company. If you orient your business thinking around ways the convenience model can benefit you and not your customer, you are missing the point. If the convenience model is going to be the primary way you orient your relationship with your Me's, then it must be focused on ways of resolving whatever inconvenience they may have in a given moment, with whatever mechanism exists, even if it doesn't result in making as much of a profit in the moment. In the extreme, it could go as far as ordering from a competitor if you're out of stock on something. Convenience means making your customers believe that you will do whatever it takes to make their lives easier.

You'd be amazed at what ingenious merchandising ideas you can come up with once you've made that mental shift toward convenience in the truest sense. If you're a toy store, for example, instead of merchandising according to type (board games, stuffed animals, action toys, etc.), maybe you could organize your products according to the age of the child. Imagine how much easier that makes it for the shopper who just wants to pop in and out of your store with an age-appropriate gift for a birthday party? Or if not by age, then at least something other than product type? Most toy buyers are what you could consider occasion shoppers, so why aren't toy stores merchandised around occasions? Because it's more convenient for your employees to restock shelves when they are organized by type (puzzles, action figures, etc.). Wrong priority if convenience is your C of choice.

The In-Convenience Store

You might think the first convenience stores should be the literal definition of this C, but they were anything but. This category of retailer earned that moniker because these stores seemed to be on every corner, so people could easily walk there to buy a loaf of bread and Kraft singles for a late-night snack. These corner stores may have charged a bit more for the essentials, but the stores were everywhere, and they were open at all hours. And that was about it.

Customers certainly were not shopping at these stores because the product assortment was good, unless they wanted only a gallon cup of sweet soda, salty snacks, or some mystery meat that had been on rollers for the past 48 hours.

Then along came Wawa, with fresh food, bright lighting, clean bathrooms, and happy associates. More than just a chain of gas station convenience stores, the privately held business (which got its start in 1902 as a dairy business that delivered milk directly to homes throughout Philadelphia) has become a beloved destination for people who want more than just a place to fill their tanks and bellies with any old greasy snack. Consumers throughout the East Coast (which is Wawa's main footprint) actually go out of their way to grab a gourmet coffee and a breakfast sandwich. Wawa consistently earns industry awards for the quality of its food and service, with its separate deli counter that does made-to-order sandwiches, and branded food and beverage products. The stores never close, and they consistently restock and clean the store throughout the day. Wawa's corporate values are "Value People, Delight Customers, and Do Things Right." The company trains its employees at Camp Wawa and Wawa University. If its associates (who, by the way, are paid well at $15 an hour or more) somehow get an order wrong, or take too long, customers get a free snack or soda.

Plug and Play

Wawa, which serves 600 million customers a year through more than 800 stores, is always trying out new technologies and formats to improve the customer experience, including its first drive-through store in Westhampton, New Jersey, late in 2020. Think about that for a second. They care a lot about selling gas. It is core to the convenience store model. But they care more about their customers and giving *them* convenience. It's constantly updating its approach with the convenience of its Me's in mind, including the option of a touch-screen ordering system for deli items, such as built-to-order salads. But it's much more than the seamless ordering of a sandwich. In a convenience-store industry where few if any invest in expensive technology, Wawa has built a third-party platform that will enable it to connect with the software of technology partners such as Uber Eats and Grubhub, allowing the company to provide door-to-door service to its customers without having to hire drivers or buy vehicles.

"We believe we have a one-of-a-kind of opportunity to enhance our relationship with people and back it up with technology to make interactions more seamless and robust," explains John Collier, Wawa's CIO.[1]

Wawa, in a technology strategy it refers to as "boundless convenience," likely has other partnerships up its sleeve that will make the consumer experience more seamless, including mobile checkouts to reduce wait times and an opt-in app that allows customers to activate the right pumps for their chosen type of gas and pay with a few clicks. The company's entire orientation is around bringing convenience back to the convenience store.

"Clean, Friendly, and in Stock"

Buc-ee's may not be as high tech, but the Texas-based chain of travel centers is just as beloved for its banks of differently positioned gas pumps numbering in the hundreds and the cleanest bathrooms along the interstates (so spotless, in fact, that they are certified). Buc-ee's corporate motto (the title of this section) should be the mantra for any company looking to give quantum consumers whatever they need in that moment in an environment that's so appealing, we're all like kids in the car screaming, "Are we there yet?" And as if Buc-ee's can read our minds, roadside signage reads, "Let us plan your next potty—52 miles," and its eponymous beaver saying, "My overbite is sexy—2 miles," as if travelers need to get any more amped up about the proximity of their most-favored pit stop.

Personally, I am so passionate about this roadside chain that I have a Buc-ee's bumper sticker on my car. To understand the appeal of Buc-ee's, you must think about the typical road-trip truck stop, where you compete with giant tractor-trailers for a handful of gas pumps and with other road trippers for parking spaces, and then choose from a selection of greasy or high-calorie foods. Then there are those bathrooms . . . Like Building 19, they are extremely convenient: just a quick right off the interstate and then right back on. Convenient, but that was it.

Until Buc-ee's redefined the category. For starters, there are no semitrucks allowed. There are acres of parking, the aforementioned gas pumps are stacked as far as the eye can see, and the gas at Buc-ee's is always cheaper than at other options nearby. But that's not all. Buc-ee's food is fresh and delicious. You can get a barbecue sandwich equal to any highly rated BBQ joint in the state and an entire zoo's worth of jerky options from its "jerky bar," but you can also get a fresh salad and other healthy menu items. As a family, we time our road-trip gas stops around breakfast and lunchtime so we can eat there instead of at one of those depressing interstate travel centers where all you can find to eat is a sad-looking hamburger or a congealed slice of pizza.

In addition to Buc-ee's vast array of snacks, including freshly made fudge from its "fudge station" and Beaver Nuggets (highly addictive caramel-coated corn pops), Buc-ee's sells cleverly merchandised cups, kids' toys, throws, baby onesies, home decor and furnishings, stuffed Buc-ee's beavers, and all manner of kitsch. There are even wines and suggested pairings to go with their food offerings.

"You want to plan your trip so that you run out of gas right there," Texas-born chef and restaurateur Ford Fry enthused to the food review website Eater.com. "Even if you're not running out of gas, you're stopping at Buc-ee's."[2]

Above all, what has led to this cultlike following of the chain, where people line up outside when new stores have their grand openings, is the associates. They have generosity of spirit to match the sheer scale of the store. No question or request from a tired traveler is too much for these folks. Their general attitude is partly explained by the fact that they are paid well, with opportunity to move up in the organization. A sign placed near one of the Buc-ee's deli counters lets everyone know how fairly the associates are paid, from $15 for a cashier, gift department associate, or warehouse associate to $19 and up for a team leader or assistant, plus a 401(k) and three weeks, paid time off for everyone.

Buc-ee's is actually less convenient than its myriad competitors because there are simply not enough locations yet, but you'd be hard-pressed to hear anyone describe their locations as *in*convenient. The company has thought through everything travelers might need or want on their journey.

Easing the Time Crunch

Like Wawa and Buc-ee's, any successful convenience model requires a mix of empathy for your Me's and what they might be going through, along with a spirit of innovation. Your customers will come back to you time and again because you are solving their problems and fulfilling needs they didn't even know they had. But if you don't, someone else surely will. Amazon has already devoured market share from millions of retailers because of the ease with which consumers can click on a product and have it delivered to their doorstep. You can even buy a car this way. Tesla allows its prospective customers to view its cars online, then delivers the vehicle they choose right to their driveway for a road test, saving them the trouble of going to the showroom (which Tesla puts in high-end malls, not along the dealer-choked highway auto-miles by the way—also for the convenience of their affluent customers) for the dreaded hard sell. And Vroom.com will do the same, but for any brand of used car.

Amazon Go is even competing with convenience stores, with physical locations that are cashierless, so that consumers can just scan the QR codes in their Amazon apps as they walk in, pick up an array of prepared foods including salads and sandwiches, and walk out. Artificial intelligence and "sensor fusion" enable the app to update your cart as you take things from the shelves or put things back. Friendly associates in orange tops stand by to help shoppers looking for something or looking confused by the "Just Walk Out Shopping" technology. Each store is costly to build, because the up-front technology investment is huge, and it doesn't offer the hot food counters of a Wawa or Buc-ee's, but the lesson for the convenience industry is this: You cannot do enough to shave off the minutes or even seconds of your time-crunched Me's.

That's partly why some of the larger traditional retail chains have begun building more of the smaller-format, neighborhood stores, where you don't have to walk hundreds of yards to find things at your local superstore. An *MIT Sloan Management Review* article predicted this trend as far back as 2000, noting how increasingly important it was for consumers to get in and get out, fast. The now-retired CEO of Walgreen's, Daniel Jorndt, called them "precision shoppers," and perfectly summed up what's been driving the convenience-model Me's: "Shopping has become a strike mission: Get in, find what you want, buy it, get out."[3]

More retailers are scrambling to figure out ways to limit or eliminate the time consumers stand in line to hand over their money. Wegmans, for example, was among the first of supermarkets to offer delivery on its prepared meals. In 2019, it announced a partnership with DoorDash to deliver its hot and cold prepared foods, or what it's calling "Wegmans Meals 2Go." The New York–based supermarket chain got the memo, seeing the double-digit increase in prepared food purchases by its Me's and taking the convenience factor further. Wegmans's customers win with more convenience options, but so does Wegmans, because it's a smart way to let customers taste-test some of the store's branded items.

Raising the Bar

Technology has forever raised the bar on how we define convenience, whether that's being able to conjure up a desired item of clothing in our size by way of an in-store, voice-activated kiosk, using data analysis to personalize a regular customer's product selection, or allowing customers to voice-order their caffeine fix through their Amazon Alexa devices so that it can be ready and paid for the instant you walk into your neighborhood Starbucks. Each new technology advancement takes the table stakes of convenience up a notch. For better or worse, consumers have come to expect instant, or almost instant, gratification, whether that's a ride that comes to them in minutes with three taps on an Uber app; a hot meal to their door from any restaurant in their city through Uber Eats, DoorDash, or Deliveroo; or their razors and shaving cream delivered within an hour through Amazon Prime.

Of course, the global pandemic accelerated this convenience trend. Because so many were avoiding shopping in brick-and-mortar stores throughout 2020, the retail industry had to come up with solutions, fast. Problem solvers like virtual showrooms and curbside pickups are quickly becoming something consumers expect in their everyday transactions rather than just some cool experimental retail trend you might come across on a visit to Silicon Valley.

Companies must make the investments that are necessary but even better if they can mutually benefit the company (but always the customer first). For example, one of the dirty little secrets of online shopping is the rate of returns, which, as the *Wall Street Journal* noted, averages around 30 percent and is much higher in certain categories and at least three times higher than items bought in a physical store.[4] So if you can offer your customer conveniences like virtual try-ons, not only are you providing a customer benefit, but you're going a long way toward mitigating the high rate of those returns. For a company to compete profitably, the convenience needs to be designed for the customer, but also connected to an operational benefit wherever possible—or you risk simply adding costs on top of costs.

Seeing Themselves

Necessity being the mother of invention, Ulta Beauty has come up with ways consumers can see themselves with a product while never leaving their couches, which is just as well, since COVID safety restrictions made it impossible to try out a lipstick shade in person. The technology allows these Me's to take a photo of themselves and overlay their features with different lipsticks, blushes, foundations, eye shadows, and so on. Or they can use one of Ulta's many stock photos of women with different shapes of faces and shades of skin or do an actual try-on through a video app that can apply hundreds of products directly onto a customer's live image. The technology, which was first offered in 2016, has really taken off since COVID, with usage increasing twelvefold between 2019 and 2020, according to the *Wall Street Journal* article.

Of course, trying on makeup virtually has fewer inherent challenges than the virtual changing room. One of the biggest challenges of buying shoes or clothing online is a lousy fit, so some retailers are investing in virtual fitting rooms, although these solutions can be hit and miss, relying on customers knowing how to measure themselves correctly, for example, and in-person 3D body scans may be too costly and far into the future. But rest assured, they are coming.

As a compromise, the *Wall Street Journal* article reports, Levi Strauss and Tommy Hilfiger have offered up digitally rendered body types, so that shoppers can see themselves in the clothes and know better which styles suit them if they have that sort of body type. The technology reduced returns by about 8 percent, according to Zeekit, the company that sells it.

Zeekit, an Israeli startup that applies military mapping technology such as real-time image processing, computer vision, and AI to fashion, has figured out how to map a person's image into thousands of segments, along with the clothing item to be "tried." Equivalent points of body and the garment are then remapped into one final simulation, taking into account the body dimensions, the fit, the size, and the fabric of the garment. Consumers can try on hundreds of outfits in a matter of minutes using the virtual topography of their bodies for a realistic simulation of fit.

Zeekit, which means "chameleon" in Hebrew, is certainly not the only technology provider trying to tackle this mash-up of customer and company benefit. And the benefit of this clear customer convenience is not just reducing returns. Many apparel and footwear retailers have come to understand that when it's easier for customers to try on—and fall in love with—more items, they are likely to buy more. So you can ship them more items, which is enormously costly, or you can leverage virtual fittings.

It's the type of innovation that syncs up perfectly with the concept of *Me*tail, putting the consumer at the heart of the story while also delivering a benefit to the company as well. That's what you want to strive for if you intend to compete on this C.

Just Keep It

Some companies are trying a less costly approach to the problem of returns that not only makes it easy for Me's, but also creates phenomenal goodwill: Keep it.

I first encountered this a few years ago when I inquired about returning an item I'd ordered on Chewy.com for one of our dogs. Instead of having us package it up, print out the return label, and take it to UPS, Chewy sent us an email note:

> Hi,
>
> I'm sorry the [product] didn't work out as expected. I've processed a refund of $37.34 to your original payment method, and that'll appear back to your account within 3–5 business days. If you feel it could still be of use, please feel free to donate it to a shelter.

If there's anything else we can help you with, feel free to reach out at any time.

Warm regards,

Tyler M.

Customer Service

Chewy

I don't even care if Tyler M. is a real person or a bot. The convenience of not having to deal with the return, along with the kindness of the suggestion to donate the item, warmed our hearts. But again, think about how smart this is for Chewy. The company delighted a customer, avoided the cost of the return, and added some goodwill into the pet universe. Returns are trending in the direction of $1 trillion a year. Another fast-growing company called Black Rifle Coffee Company follows a similar model, and when I needed to exchange a shirt for a different size, they told me to donate the original to a veterans' organization, first responder, or similar organization rather than send it back. Another goodwill creating moment that reinforced what the brand stands for with perfect circularity.

The industry-wide waste, of time, cardboard, fossil fuel, and so much more, boggles the mind. By some estimates, upward of 5 percent of returned goods actually end up in a landfill because retailers simply can't figure out a better way to handle them. Even when they are resold, returns cost billions in restocking, warehousing, and shipment fees, not to mention the added cost of managing the customer experience. Even Amazon and Walmart are taking a page out of Chewy and Black Rifle Coffee's book and (selectively) letting customers keep or donate the products. Depending on the price of the item, there is a certain threshold at which it is simply not worth the time and money to process the return. But Chewy and Black Rifle Coffee's genius was to turn this clear company cost into a customer convenience, that would in turn benefit the company with more goodwill and loyalty. And its gesture made us feel cared for and understood, whatever their motives were for the bottom line.

There are countless examples of using convenience as customer benefit that also is good for the bottom line. Take Pret-a-Manger, which began giving consumers the option to buy coffee on a monthly subscription basis. The international sandwich shop franchise realized that subscribing once for something that you use or consume on a regular basis is more convenient than pulling out your credit card, cash, or phone every time you want to pay. Imagine if you had to buy each show individually on Netflix? People would never do it, or not as much of it. Or pay for every Peloton class you take? And so on. But Pret understood that the ease of transaction through a subscription service can work even and especially for a high-margin consumable like coffee. So this clear customer benefit versus the more conventional pay-by-the-drink approach has the advantage of being a customer convenience that won't take a bite out of Pret's bottom line because of the margin inherent in selling brown water and more likely increase customer loyalty because of the subscription. Now think, what opportunities do you have to do this for your business?

Strategy Versus Table Stake

Experiencing the ease of a transaction doesn't necessarily have to leave Me's feeling warm and fuzzy about their relationship with you. It's not as if Costco's gas hose extension comes from a place of caring about my personal happiness or the desire to build a personal connection with me. It's making my life easier because it shortens the amount of time I spend in line getting gas, which in turn multiplies the number of other Me's getting gas at the Costco pump, ultimately increasing the company's profits exponentially.

So it's important to distinguish between convenience and what is often mistaken for convenience: customer service. Building relationships with your customers through customer service—through courtesy, caring, compassion, and curiosity about your Me's—is not a C. You don't have to provide excellent customer service, and companies can be successful with or without it if they adhere to their special recipe of Cs. Whatever C model you happen to be focused on, the level of customer service you provide is a choice. This is the difference between a strategy and a tactic. By all means, engineer your operations precisely so that you can provide an appropriate level of service, whether that's increasing wages or providing a level of associate training that teaches accountability. Help employees to understand what it means to go above and beyond. But recognize that outcaring the competition is not, in itself, a competitive strategy. You still need to build your business around one, or more, of the Cs, and the convenience model can be particularly powerful if done from the customer's perspective.

For an example of a convenience strategy that might have been a bit off the mark, consider the example of Kohl's, which in 2018 partnered with Amazon to become a drop-off location for Amazon returns. Amazon has many customer benefits, but ease of returns is not one of them. Sure, it can get stuff to you fast, but if you want to return stuff to Amazon, the burden is on you. Amazon addresses this logistical inconvenience through Amazon lockers, UPS drop-off locations, and partnerships with certain retailers. When the partnership with Kohl's was first announced, there were shockwaves throughout retail because here was a direct competitor offering to partner with the online giant. It was a bold move by both companies. When the program was first rolled out, it was tested in a handful of stores, and Kohl's put the return location right at the front of the test stores, ensuring that the location was as convenient as possible. As one might expect, customers loved it, and it drove a lot of traffic to those specific Kohl's locations.

Here was a clear and obvious convenience for the Amazon customer. But it was also a way for Kohl's to say to its customers that it understands them and that if Kohl's can help by turning two trips into one, it wanted to be part of the convenience in their customers' lives. The test run was so successful that in 2019, Kohl's announced that it was rolling out the benefit to all stores. What a win for the convenience C, right? Not so fast. When Kohl's rolled out nationwide, it made a critical change, locating the drop off locations deeper inside the stores.

I wasn't there, but you can imagine the internal conversations prior to the rollout went something like this: "Our customers love this convenience, but we aren't making any money since customers just come in, drop and go. What if we put the drop-off at the back of the store? That way people would have to walk through the store to get there, and if they walk all the way to the back of our store, they'll pass a lot of stuff and may buy something!"

Likely they had beautifully made presentations from a top-tier consulting firm to show what would happen to their "attach rate" (corporate-speak for "How much more stuff can we make a customer buy?"). But Kohl's forgot the first rule of convenience: It can only be a competitive strategy if it's convenient for your customer, not for you.

So a convenience benefit, one that was lauded as innovative and groundbreaking, become an *in*convenience. Kohl's customers do still make Amazon returns, but they know that they are being used as "attach-rate bait." Which brings me back to my original point: If you are planning a convenience strategy and you find yourself imagining all the ways it can benefit you, stop right there. There are many mutually beneficial conveniences, but conveniences tilted in the company's favor will do nothing to endear you to your Me's looking for convenience and may even hurt your relationship with them. Of course Kohl's has many positive attributes and customer benefits and talking about this decision may seem like nit-picking but it is a perfect example of what I see far too often—company-centric thinking masquerading as customer centric.

Me's know what's really going on. They don't object if something you're doing increases sales, but only if it makes their lives easier in the process. Again, in the convenience model, anything you do from the supply chain all the way up to the checkout and the return process must solve *their* problem, not yours. So just be willing to call it what it really is. If you're a luxury store that offers a personal shopping service, you are no doubt offering it as a convenience to your customer. But if you only show products you are selling, what you are offering your consumers is a "personal seller," not a personal shopper. That's fine, of course, but a personal shopper would be able to sell items your company doesn't even carry.

Botched BOPIS

Another annoyance is how something specifically designed for convenience is often poorly executed when a company hasn't adequately oriented itself around that purpose. Consider convenience innovations such as curbside pickup or buy online, pick up in store (BOPIS).

The system works well if when I walk into the store, it's obvious where I need to go to pick up an order, and the order is ready and waiting for me. But too often, the pickup is also in the back of the store, or it's merged with the customer service desk, so I have to wait in a line of people trying to return something without a receipt and so on. Businesses can choose any operating model they want, but unless every aspect of your operating model reinforces your Cs, you're off course. Put it wherever you want, by all means; just don't pretend to yourself or anyone else that it is the convenience model if it's not, in fact, convenient.

To give you an idea of what that feels like from the consumer's perspective, let me share with you a recent experience I had picking up an order at a national restaurant chain. The location I went to is in a mall, but it has its own entrance. When I logged into the online ordering system, I saw lots of graphics and copy implying that it would be as simple as pulling up to the curb to have my order handed to me. But when I arrived, there was no signage letting me know where to park or pull up.

I went to the valet stand, where the staff allowed me to leave my car for a few minutes free of charge, ran into the restaurant, and was made to wait in line with customers looking to be seated at a table. Finally, I was able to get the attention of a waiter, who told me that the pickup location was in the back by the kitchen. I made my way there and found a pile of bags waiting to be picked up by Grubhub and Uber Eats drivers. After digging through more than 20 bags, I found mine. I could not have designed a more inconvenient convenience, and I have not been to or ordered from this restaurant chain since.

If you're going to offer something that purportedly makes the customer's experience more convenient, why not go all the way? It may seem odd to think of Costco as a convenience player. After all, it sells packages of toilet paper taller than many children. But the customer service desk is right at the front of the store. If you need to process a return, Costco employees take it back with a smile, and you can choose to go in and shop more, or just walk out. I'm certain Costco's management has done the math and knows that the numbers support moving the desk to the back, and yet for Costco, a pinch of convenience is part of its chosen recipe.

Again, convenience can most assuredly serve both you and your Me, even with an eye on "the numbers." Consider, for example, a lesser-known option than BOPIS: BOSTS (buy online, ship to store). It works especially well for apparel companies as opposed to, say, an electronics store where a customer picks up a toaster or computer either through curbside delivery or BOPIS and then leaves. For footwear, apparel, and other retailers besides, BOSTS is something that should be leveraged, but too many companies lump BOSTS into the BOPIS category. They see it as just another option to offer instead of one to highlight and promote, which is shortsighted.

Why? Because if a customer comes into your store, you've saved on shipping the item to their home (in retail parlance, it "rides free" along with other merchandise already being shipped to a store). It usually also helps avoid paying for return shipping and processing given the high rates of returns in those categories, not to mention the time that returned product sits in a distribution center before you can process the product and resell it. When you bring customers to your store and they don't like what they ordered, you at least have a shot at finding the right size or a different item, or perhaps even adding to the sale, assuming it's convenient for those customers.

Even if you don't make a sale and the customer just opts to return the item, the merchandise stays right in the store and can be resold quickly. Since BOSTS lowers your costs, why not present it as a customer benefit first, perhaps by offering discounts on BOSTS orders, for example? As long as it truly is a convenience for your consumer, it's fine for a benefit to go both ways. Or, why not Reserve Online Review in Store (RORIS)? So I could pick three black attaché cases online, schedule an appointment, and come into a store where they would be waiting for me to choose one (or none) but saving me precious time. The easier you make it for your Me's, the better for you, regardless of motive.

Added Ingredients

Convenience can take courage. Consider Target again. Its deal with Ulta Beauty is another convenience enhancement for both retail brands. Late in 2020, they formed a strategic partnership to open 100 Ulta Beauty "shops in shop" (of 1,000 square feet each), located next to Target's own beauty department, with consultation areas staffed by Target employees trained by Ulta. Target customers will also have access to Ulta's GLAMlab virtual try-on digital tool.

While it may seem counterintuitive to bring in a product segment competitor, the bet is that Target's and Ulta's Me's will appreciate the convenience of one-stop shopping. Instead of having to drive to another store, they can have the Ulta experience while also picking up paper goods and groceries at their local Target, even if these Ulta spaces have been scaled down from the usual 10,000 square feet to 1,000 square feet. By locating inside a Target, Ulta is meeting its customers where they are. Target, meanwhile, gets to upscale its offerings with the prestige beauty brands Ulta carries, just as it did by opening in-store Disney shops at certain locations. In effect, the teaming up of Ulta Beauty and Target creates a tide that lifts both boats. To get there required both companies to truly focus on their Cs and not let "the numbers" get in the way.

"This is more about new shopping occasions that we can capture," explained Mary Dillon, Ulta's CEO. "Beauty in our home format is a deep, immersive experience. . . . Guests need to shop for other needs and there is a convenience need."[5] Ulta, like Target, has, of course, picked more than one C, but it is clear that both have decided to season their recipe with a heavy dash of convenience.

Another example of a multifaceted C player doing something similar is Nordstrom's New York flagship. Nordstrom has always been known for a high level of convenience and service. But to compete in New York City by curating luxury fashion, accessories, cosmetics, and decor, the company has clearly decided it needs to do more, including overinvesting to create as many conveniences as possible for its customers, including—before the pandemic—getting their dinner ordered or being able to get their hair and nails done in the store as part of its beauty services. There's a concierge service that will call you a cab, book you a restaurant, and give you an umbrella if it's raining. Nordstrom even offers in-store express alterations and shoe repairs. It also takes returns from other online retailers for you.

Not all the services are free, of course. Nordstrom's Me's pay extra for the in-store blowout, for example. But the retailer has taken one-stop shopping to a whole new level, allowing harried New Yorkers to take care of all their time-sucking errands inside one luxurious, stress-free location.

These conveniences cost Nordstrom, too. But over time, the company can build up a powerful base of loyal customers. By contrast, let's look at Neiman Marcus, which opened its first store in New York City around the same time as Nordstrom. The company located its main entrance on the fifth floor of a hulking mall on the far west side of Midtown Manhattan, all but saying to their Me's, "We know you love us so much you'll endure crosstown traffic and a five-floor elevator ride just for the privilege of shopping with us." Neiman Marcus closed that location in 2020 during its bankruptcy.

Items in Your Cart

Put yourself in the shoes of your Me's. Think of all the little things that make the transaction as smooth and pleasurable as possible.

Convenience is in the eye of the customer, *not* the company. If the convenience model is going to be the primary way you orient your relationship with your Me's, then you should focus your whole being on ways of resolving whatever inconvenience they may have in a given moment, even if it doesn't result in making a profit. Think of it as a long-term investment in the relationship with your consumers. Do whatever it takes to fulfill the needs and desires of your Me's with the least hassle for them, not you.

Leverage innovation to create "boundless convenience." Constantly update your approach with the convenience of your Me's in mind, whether that's a touch-screen ordering system or curbside pickup.

A successful convenience model requires empathy for your Me's. Your customers will come back to you time and again because you are solving their problems and fulfilling needs they didn't even know they had. If you don't, someone else will.

Do all you can to save them precious time. Shopping has become a strike mission: Get in, find what you want, buy it, and get out. You cannot do enough to shave off the minutes or even seconds of your time-crunched Me's.

A convenience can be beneficial to both you and your Me's. It doesn't have to just be good for your customer. Technology such as virtual mirrors syncs up perfectly with the concept of *Me*tail, putting the consumers at the heart of the story while making it easier to fill their baskets and press "click." Even allowing customers to keep or donate a product has a business benefit. It builds your brand and creates goodwill.

Don't confuse customer service with convenience. Building relationships with customers through courtesy, caring, compassion, and curiosity about your Me's is not a C. It is a tactic, albeit an important one.

Convenience on its own may not be enough. Consider combining convenience with other Cs. For example, if you can't attract customers with price, make yourself more convenient than others selling similar wares. Whatever ingredients you pick, and however you combine them, be sure you have a product and pricing strategy to support that flavor profile.

Your cart total: *Convenience!*

Proceed to next chapter . . .

6

CATEGORY EXPERT: SHOW ME WHAT YOU KNOW

If you have knowledge, let others light their candles in it.

—MARGARET FULLER, EARLY NINETEENTH-CENTURY
AMERICAN JOURNALIST

It was uncanny.

Every time I needed some obscure type of screw, switch, or hinge, the team at my hometown hardware store—Elliott's—knew exactly what I needed and where in the store's many aisles of fasteners to find it. The salespeople would go to just the right place in just the right aisle, pull out a drawer filled with the thingamajigs covered in decades' worth of dust, take one out, explain exactly where and how to install it, then charge me all of 18 cents. They saved me hours of frustration on the countless occasions I ordered something online for self-assembly only to find a piece of hardware was missing.

It was always worth the trip to the store, purely because of the staff's encyclopedic knowledge of all things hardware and the store's incredible range of products. I could always trust I would get exactly what I needed when I needed it. Despite the ease of ordering something from my armchair on Amazon or the illusion of saving money at a hardware superstore, by not getting it right the first time without Elliott's onsite expertise, I'd often buy the wrong thing and have to return it, so having this shop as my go-to was a no-brainer.

Elliott's is a terrific example of the "category expert." The *category expert model* of retail is based on being the most knowledgeable and the best stocked with a range of anything Me's can possibly need in a specific realm—in this case, the realm of home improvement. McGuckin Hardware in Boulder, Colorado, is another example of a business that has become a destination for the depth of associate expertise, along with a vast array of products. In fact, McGuckin, with 60,000 square feet of sales floor, selling more than 200,000 items, with 250 associates serving customers in 18 different departments, from garden and housewares to plumbing and automotive, has been able to carry the model over into a much larger assortment than that of Elliott's or your typical hardware store.

Like many successful category experts, McGuckin started small when in 1955 Llewellyn Commodore "Bill" McGuckin, a rugged mountain man, set up shop with four people running four departments. As the store's website states, old Bill was a firm believer in "personalized service, selection, and first-hand experience"—a philosophy he drummed into his son-in-law, Dave Hight, who became his partner in the store as the two men built it.

Understanding that category expertise cannot reside within just a handful of people, nor can it be contained within a single generation, McGuckin continually scoured the region for talent and experience. Today, each store department has a "green vest": a category expert who walks the aisles. These individuals are approachable and friendly, always ready to help and advise consumers wandering the Grilling and Outdoor Living department, for example, who look like they might be overwhelmed about how to open, much less use, the Big Green Egg.

McGuckin also offers courses, empowering its Me's to become their own experts and build it themselves, whether that's a birdhouse, a composting system, or an outdoor kitchen. Elliott's also teaches its Me's the basics through online and in-store classes. In fact, Elliott's has one of my favorite online classes of all time: Toilets 101. The point is, the company manifests its category expertise in all the ways one might want to interact with a category expert—through the products, to be sure, but also the sense that I, too, can obtain a certain level of expertise.

The Edges of the Bell Curve

Make no mistake. Elliott's—which has five locations in the Dallas Metroplex in 2021—is no Home Depot or Lowe's, and neither is McGuckin. Unlike the big-box category killers, which sell the most commonly sought items, the true category experts work around the edges of the bell curve, providing specialty items that most volume sellers do not. They sell the core products as well, but their advantage is gained on the margin. It's not enough to have everything in a given category. They must also *know* everything about their category. And for that one-in-a-million question that stumps them, they must know where to find the answer.

The challenges of getting this right means that this C is not for everyone. In fact, among the six Cs, it's probably going to be the least popular, at least in its purest form. From sporting goods to electronics to beauty products, the category expert model of *Me*tail enables significant flexibility, but it also requires focused investment only on the things that represent expertise to your Me's. Stray too far, and your Me's will not believe you. For this C, you need to have knowledgeable store associates, access to product information, and installation and repair assistance—not as an afterthought or through an outsourced partner, but as a built-in part of company culture. These are areas that demonstrate expertise to Me's. This also means that it is difficult to do beyond a certain range of related products. It's one thing to trust McGuckin for plumbing supplies, outdoor grills, pool supplies, auto parts, and such. But what about computers? Or drones? Or artisanal coffee beans? Probably not.

For this reason, category expertise is somewhat limiting, at least under the same company banner. There's nothing to prevent a true believer in category expertise from opening a range of companies, all of which would be category experts in their own right. But again, don't push it and risk stretching your customer's credulity.

This C also requires the most investment in frontline associates and inventory that may not sell very often. You need to invest more resources into your frontline associates and store management because it is *their* intellectual capital and skill sets, oftentimes more than the actual merchandise you are selling, that is attracting and keeping your consumers. The internet also makes it much harder to be a category expert because information and products can be sourced from countless sites. However, there is still no YouTube video that can compete with a live demonstration of how something should work when you're truly stuck. Your business must be the first place consumers think of when they have a problem that needs to be solved. Your Me's need to have a sense of urgency to get up off their couches and visit you.

Though most of us may never set foot in one, try to conjure an image of your typical neighborhood skateboard shop. They tend to be owned and staffed by individuals who live and breathe the skater lifestyle. Their Me's tend to be fellow boarders in the neighborhood who already know a lot. Average consumers would be terrified of walking into one of these places, fearing they'd be made fun of by the cool kids. That's why we haven't seen a national chain of skater category experts. They possess a local expertise that attracts a finite number of Me's (the skateboard set), but that set is also disdainful of people who do not live the lifestyle; so extend a skate shop brand too far, and your Me's will no longer find you credible.

Killing the Category Killers

For decades, big-box category killers obliterated small neighborhood stores. Category killers provided average service, an average range of products, and an average experience. Their competitive model was basically to accumulate stuff inside a cavernous space. If you've read this far, you can see why that's not going to work as well in a *Me*tail world. They stock products under the bell curve, locating their stores in large off-mall locations, in the hope that will be enough to attract the sheer volume of consumers it takes to make a profit with this model.

And the formula worked, for a period of time. Book chains like Barnes & Noble and Borders ate up the small neighborhood bookstores. Local music and movie stores got razed by Blockbuster, HMV, Tower Records, and Virgin Megastores. Toys R Us ravaged the mom-and-pop toy stores. Until a new model emerged: the category killer *killer,* called Amazon. You see, killing a category is a strategy that could work for only so long.

Best Buy was also a category killer at one point, but unlike the aforementioned retailers, it realized (before it was too late) that killing categories is not a viable long-term strategy and went all-in to become a category expert. Going back a few years at the height of Amazon's competitive strength in electronics and computers, if you walked into a Best Buy, it was nearly impossible to find a sales associate who could explain why a certain laptop was better or guide you through the purchase of a home entertainment system. That was because, in an effort to plug the company's profitability hole, Best Buy executives cut cost after cost without regard for the effect on the customers.

I remember a time when I asked a question about one of the dozens of printer models in the store and was answered with a shrug: true story. Then, in 2012, Best Buy did something unthinkable. It hired Hubert Joly, a CEO who had no retail experience, although he did have his own personal experience as a Me. He began a multiyear campaign to fix the company, leaning heavily on the category expert model. Best Buy reshaped its entire approach and cost structure to become a place where customers could ask questions and get experience-based answers. While the smart money left Best Buy for dead like all the other category killers swallowed up by Amazon, a funny thing happened. The Me's came back.

This allowed Best Buy to pivot toward more expertise and value-added services, and that emphasis on expertise is precisely what saved it from obsolescence.

Renew Blue

When Joly took the wheel, the French executive immediately set about finding ways to reinvest in expertise. He acquired the

Geek Squad, Best Buy's version of Apple's Genius Bar, only arguably more accessible because the Geek Squad made house calls. It was all part of Joly's move to double down on differentiation with highly trained and qualified store associates and superior product selection, calling this transformation "Renew Blue."

Without the benefit of my *Me*tail vocabulary, Joly did exactly what I am exhorting you all to do in this book: Identify your C or Cs and reorient your entire company toward that goal. Choose and focus. The impact of his actions could be seen within a matter of months, and by 2013, the once-stumbling chain of stores saw its stock triple.

Of course, Renew Blue wasn't just about category expertise. The Geek Squad and better associates was never going to be the only draw for Best Buy's Me's. People used to treat the retailer as a kind of electronics showroom, touching and feeling the products they were thinking about buying, then going home to order them on Amazon or some other website where they could get a cheaper price. Sometimes they even ordered the items on their phones while still inside the store! But Joly effectively added the cost model to his overall strategy, pricing the most highly compared products at the lowest price so that no one walking into a Best Buy had a reason to buy anywhere else.

At the same time, Best Buy radically reshaped its corporate cost structure to allow the company to invest in these changes. After deciding which of the six Cs belonged to its turnaround strategy, the company was relentless in focusing on them, making difficult decisions and ignoring all the other shiny objects. Price itself was not the objective, but Joly knew that price perception was a stumbling block, and so he addressed it. He was implementing what is often called the "bread, milk, and eggs" model: making sure that you are sharply priced on everyday items, where your shopper knows the competitive pricing landscape all too well.

"Our goal is not to be lower than the competition," Joly told the *New York Times* for an article aptly titled "Underdog Against Amazon, Best Buy Charges Ahead." Rather, it was to offer "a very compelling set of customer promises with the assortment, the advice, the convenience, the service. So, our goal is simply to eliminate price as an obstacle to buying."[1]

Flipping the Script

Joly leaned into the idea of Best Buy as an expert and converted foot traffic into customers with the store's own special blend of expert service. In so doing, he flipped the script on Amazon. Best Buy even formed an exclusive strategic partnership with Amazon to sell its Fire televisions and other hardware that's part of the Alexa ecosystem while also becoming a third-party seller in the Amazon marketplace. It was a deal that Amazon needed more than Best Buy because Amazon needed a brick-and-mortar space with knowledgeable salespeople to demonstrate its Amazon-branded products. (Other brands, including Samsung and Apple, also began partnerships.)

"Best Buy is the most important U.S. retailer for consumer electronics. Everyone who wants to sell products like this comes to Best Buy—Amazon is no exception," commented Stephen Baker, a technology industry advisor at market research firm NDP group, at the time of the deal. "If you have large-hardware brand aspirations, you have to sell through Best Buy, and they know how to leverage their strength with their partners."[2]

Best Buy has since been using its dominant position as a category expert to broaden its areas of specialty, including partnering with Apple on repair services. It also caught up with emerging trends by growing its health and technology segment, including home fitness tools and medical devices, thus listening to its customers and paying attention to the various ways they wanted to use this technology in their lives. In 2018 (in what now seems like a prescient move, given the pandemic), the retail giant acquired GreatCall, Inc., a provider of healthcare technology and personal emergency-response services to elderly consumers.

GreatCall is perhaps best known for the easy-to-use Jitterbug mobile phone that you may have bought for your technology-phobic aging parents or grandparents. Its products also happen to be a lifeline to more than 900,000 senior subscribers who use their connected devices to easily reach medical professionals. It says a lot that Best Buy's Geek Squad teams will be entrusted with explaining the technology to this growing group of Me's, who are often overlooked by consumer companies.

Servicing these consumers in store and setting up these devices in their homes required next-level expertise and customer service. It would take patience and understanding to support these users, who've spent much of their time on this planet living without technology and are often unfamiliar with terms many of us take for granted. But with the US population of 65-and-overs expected to grow to 75 million by 2040, the GreatCall acquisition was a smart business move, especially if Best Buy continues to invest in its associates' expertise and interpersonal skills.

Does Best Buy offer the expertise of, say, a local home entertainment store that sells state-of-the-art equipment? Perhaps not. No one is going to confuse Best Buy with an absolute expert such as World Wide Stereo in Montgomeryville, Pennsylvania, or Paragon Sight and Sound in Ann Arbor, Michigan. But average consumers who aren't necessarily in the market for a tricked-out, top-of-the-line home theater can at least rest assured that Best Buy is a place they can go to online or offline, pick up what they need, and find someone who can explain the differences among various options and how to use them.

Sufficiently Knowledgeable

Don't be overly intimidated by this C, because there are many levels of expertise that can work for this model . . . within reason. Like Target, Wegmans has selected multiple Cs in varying amounts, and it also offers enough category expertise to satisfy most consumers. If you go to Wegmans's beer department, you can expect the associate in charge to have tasted most of the brews and be able to recommend something you might like. At Total Wines, which sells a breadth of other types of alcohol, you won't have to look far to find someone who can answer questions about the dryness of a Prosecco or the aging of a particular bourbon. At Williams Sonoma, someone is going to know about which Dutch oven you should buy or offer you a fine salmon recipe for your air fryer. The point is, to compete on this C means to have *enough* expertise for your Me's. How much depends on how broad or narrow you want to be.

Cultivate a Following

Paradoxically, the deeper you embed expertise in your business, the tougher it is to scale. But since this book is for all consumer companies, it's worth noting how powerful this C can be for a neighborhood business with no aspirations to have a store in every mall or strip center. A case in point: Chambers Street Wines in Lower Manhattan. Here's what one reviewer for *New York Magazine*'s food and wine blog, *Grub Street*, has to say about the wine shop it rates the best in New York: "The shop eschews score-bearing placards and adjective soups from third-party critics in favor of conversation, and at least one person on duty will know a detail or two about the weather in Tourmont or the slate in the soil, or even the cool dog that patrols the vines."[3]

It's a different kind of consumer who seeks out a wine shop like Chambers Street Wines. Its level of category expert cultivates a market of Me's that's so narrow, it needs to build long-lasting relationships with its dedicated oenophiles. To that end, the shop sends out regular email blasts that give the latest news about its collection of vintage burgundies; provides interviews with an Italian vintner about his Barolos; notifies customers about wine tastings; or highlights a particularly special bottle of wine, such as its Château Sègue-Longue Monnier 2011 Médoc instead of whatever wine the giant houses are pushing. Me's have an almost infinite choice of places to buy their expensive wines in New York City, but they go to Chambers Street to spend their money almost entirely because of the cult following the store has built through its informative yet down-to-earth conversations with them.

Again, when you're at that level of category expertise (and, to some extent, curation), your knowledge of what you are selling to your Me's must be so on point, enhancing their experience and opening their eyes to the wonders of your product, that your Me's go out of their way to engage with you and your associates. These consumers wouldn't even think of seeking out a service or buying that particular product from anyone else. You have built that foundation of trust that you know your stuff, and for that reason, your business maintains a steady and loyal following of Me's.

For another—and nearby—example, if you're Murray's Cheese Shop in Greenwich Village, about a mile and a half to the north of Chambers Street Wine, your customers may be buying a creamy Cypress Grove Truffle Tremor chèvre from you not necessarily because they can't get it anywhere else, but because of the wealth of knowledge they know they'll get from the cheese monger behind the counter, who will cheerfully slice you a sample as she mentally prepares you for the velvety tang you're about to experience on your tongue.

These category experts have stood the test of time (in Murray's case, 75 years) and weathered the retail apocalypse because of the unparalleled depth of their knowledge. They have become destinations not only for locals but for national and international consumers, and they've broadened their footprints through e-commerce. Through its "CheezE-mails," Murray's (like the wine shop) keeps its Me's well informed about its selection of cheeses; their provenance; appropriate pairings with wine, fruit, and charcuterie; the cheeses that are best for grilling; and the cheese that makes the best fondue. Again, like the best category experts, Murray's empowers its Me's with online and in-person courses on such topics as arranging cheese boards and making the perfect mac 'n' cheese. The cheese retailer even offers a Murray's Boot Camp: three days of lectures, demonstrations, and tastings that will leave its graduates so cheese literate, they will be able to differentiate and describe different cheese styles and pair them like a pro.

Revenge of the Mom-and-Pops

Much like the curators, category experts in the classic sense tend to be smaller stores or smaller chains, but they've been enjoying a resurgence in the *Me*tail economy. You might even say they're the mom-and-pops' revenge on all those big category-killer chains that once wiped out so many beloved neighborhood businesses. They are small but mighty, like New York City's Madame Paulette Dry Cleaners, which bills itself as "The World's Leading Cleaning and Restoration Specialists for Over Half a Century." There are thousands of dry cleaning and tailoring shops throughout New York City. But Madame Paulette is the go-to place if you spilled red wine on your Christian Dior couture gown or need detailing on the tablecloths in your private jet. It's where people who care deeply about preserving the fabric of their treasured clothing and interior decor go not just for a rescue but for long-term care.

This company's Me's are willing to pay top dollar because they trust the experts at Madame Paulette to know exactly which chemicals or agents can break down a mustard stain in that beloved crisp white linen blouse or how to remove the oil blotch from those elbow-length calfskin Sermoneta gloves or exactly where to source the sequins, seed pearls, or brass buttons that need to be replaced on the lapel of an Yves Saint Laurent jacket. Even something decades old that's been yellowed or oxidized with age, like Joe DiMaggio's baseball jersey, has been made to look brand new with this expert's careful hand-cleaning.

As its own website boasts, Madame Paulette is "a place where shirts are treated like the Shroud of Turin." And designer Vera Wang swears it's "the only establishment I trust to maintain, renew, and preserve my bridal collection."

The owner of Madame Paulette is John Mahdessian, who is known as the "Sultan of Stains" (second in great nicknames only to the groundskeeper I met at a Little League baseball complex in Tyler, Texas, who called himself the Marquis de Sod). Mahdessian comes from a family that has been in the cleaning business for more than 70 years. His customers are made up of fashionistas and Manhattan socialites. He keeps a vault for *Vogue* editor Anna Wintour's clothes and cleans the costumes of the Radio City Music Hall Rockettes.

But it's not the high profiles of Mahdessian's Me's that have kept his business going while one in six cleaners in New York City permanently shuttered during the work-from-home era. It is that extreme level of expertise that Madame Paulette's customers know they could not get anywhere else.

Selling the Great Outdoors

A great example of a category expert at medium scale is the every-thing-related-to-camping company REI Co-op, an outdoor retailer headquartered just outside Seattle, which has 168 locations and is the country's largest consumer co-op, with more than 19 million subscribers. Outdoor-oriented Me's can walk in and not only find anything they might need to climb a rockface in Maine or set up a tent in sequoia country, but also get trustworthy advice on whether they are better off purchasing the Flexlock or Sabretooth Pro Crampons. Whatever they are thinking about doing in the outdoors, there is someone at REI to talk them through the entire experience. Of course, they'll likely walk out having made several purchases, but the crash course, advice, and expertise are the bonus gift that also ensures Me's don't waste a lot of money on the wrong items.

But REI offers its Me's much more than just expert advice on which outdoor products to buy. REI combines its category exper-tise with another C, community, in order to, as it says on its web-site, "build on the infrastructure that makes outside life possible," and the company invests millions a year in hundreds of nonprofits that steward and create access to places of rugged, natural beauty. Wherever the co-op has a physical location, it hosts beginner- to advanced-level workshops, where its Me's can learn, for instance, tips for backpacking through Yosemite National Park from profes-sionally trained instructors.

REI's experts also curate adventure-travel experiences for their millions of Me's. REI runs more than 200 itineraries around the world, and in 2020, it expanded its domestic offerings for lock-down-weary families craving the outdoors for some safe and socially distanced hiking and cycling, making concessions to those who might prefer to sleep in a lodge as opposed to under the stars. These choices are self-reinforcing, as the more people get outdoors, the more opportunities they have to interact with REI's experts.

The lesson here is that when you establish and maintain your expertise, it creates a level of trust that allows you to expand in different directions, but again only so far. Nobody would believe REI if the company started selling tuxedoes, for example. The key is to never dilute that front line of knowledgeable associates. And if you can't offer the same depth of expertise as an REI rock-climbing expert or a Murray's cheese monger or a Madame Paulette stain remover, you must be prepared to introduce more Cs into your recipe with the same level of thought and care.

Personal Passion

Perhaps the definition of category expert at full scale is the beauty retail chain Sephora, which operates more than 2,700 stores in 35 countries around the world. The company, which itself is more of an aggregator of the best brands in everything from skin care and lipstick to hair care, was founded back in 1970. It began with an open-sell retail concept, where products are displayed out in the open instead of behind counters (an innovation in beauty retail at the time), with carefully curated brands grouped into logical sections of the store (a dash of convenience). But it was the unbiased expertise of the well-trained store associates, who guide consumers through not only the tried-and-true beauty brands but also indie darlings, emerging favorites, and Sephora's own line, that won their Me's.

A shopper who walks in and asks a store associate to help her find the right products for her skin, for example, will be guided through a range of products rather than pushed to a certain brand. The associates are trained to find what's best for their Me's based on their in-depth knowledge of how the various moisturizers, astringents, and face oils perform on skin types. Short of going to the dermatologist, the Sephora customer won't find a better or more impartial recommendation.

What's striking about Sephora is the passion that seems to go along with the expertise, which cascades down from the top management to the shop floor, where cashiers wear the very products they're checking out for consumers with the flourish of makeup artists. The sales associates recommend based on personal experience as well as a depth of knowledge, as do the in-house category experts who comb the world for products, form exclusive partnerships with niche beauty brands, plan store promotions, train floor staff, and educate consumers. Sephora does a series on YouTube called "Sephora Edit: Scouted by Us, Chosen by You" to show its Me's the various personalities along with the levels of expertise of those working behind the scenes to curate and advise.

One "Edit" featured Elodie Canestrier, a category manager at Sephora in Singapore who specializes in hair care. The French-born employee, who had been working at Sephora's South East Asia regional office for three years, answers questions about her own hair-care concerns and preferences; and her detailed knowledge of the brands, their ingredients, smells, textures, and how they solve various hair problems is jaw-dropping. You can tell from the specificity of her responses that she lives and breathes these products, from the detoxing scalp serum she uses weekly for her sensitive scalp to the peach- and rose-scented mask she slathers on her hair when it gets dry from overprocessing.

To be a category expert, you must be able to attract employees like Elodie to your front lines. Your strategy depends on those face-to-face interactions with credible, knowledgeable associates. You must be all-in on where you invest your resources, which for this C means your people and their ability to show their Me's how things work. Sephora made that commitment. It also recognized that to attract and retain the right people—bright, young, and enthusiastic—it needed to build an appealing workplace culture. Sephora has been recognized by *Forbes* magazine as one of "America's Best Employers" three years running, in 2018, 2019, and 2020, with

83 percent of employees saying it's a great place to work, compared with 59 percent at a typical US company.

Attracting more Me's also requires frontline staff who are as diverse as they are. In 2019 and 2020, Sephora scored 100 percent on the Human Rights Campaign's Corporate Quality Index, the national benchmarking tool on corporate policies and practices pertinent to LGBTQ+ employees. Not only does Sephora attract Millennial talent with these policies; it's proving that diversity and inclusion is good for business through its promotion of Black-owned businesses. It became the first large retailer to take the 15 Percent Pledge, where 15 percent of its brand assortment will go to Black-owned businesses, and it recently launched an industry initiative to combat racial bias in stores.[4]

The litmus test for this C is to make it easy for your Me's to find people who know what they are talking about. The depth and scope of knowledge is up to you. But access to someone on your front line with useful knowledge of some kind is nonnegotiable. That's not a high bar, but you'd be surprised how many companies trip and fall over it. They've been getting rid of full-time associates in the effort to cut costs, which might be OK for a different C, but not for this one. Part-time workers turn over 100 percent or more within a given year, so there's simply no continuity of knowledge.

To compete in this C at any level of expertise, there is no way around it: More so than the other Cs, you must invest in your entire ecosystem, from the frontline staff to your e-commerce platform to customer service across the board. You will always need that core group of employees, from floor staff to managers like Elodie, who live to impart their knowledge to enrich the lives of their Me's, whether that's directing them to the perfect serum to control frizz or the right gloves to wear on their next Everest expedition.

Items in Your Cart

It's not enough to have everything in a given category. Category experts live in the product margins, to be sure. But they must also know everything about their category. And for that one-in-a-million question that stumps them, they must know who does have the answer.

Mastery of information is the key, as is the specialization of products and services that consumers won't be able to easily access elsewhere. Category expertise can be flexible in terms of the products or services you offer, but it requires focused investment on the things that represent expertise: Knowledgeable store associates, access to product information, and installation assistance cannot be afterthoughts. You need to build in these elements as part of the company culture.

Invest in your people. Invest more resources into your frontline associates and store management because it is their intellectual capital and skill sets, oftentimes more than the actual merchandise you are selling, that is attracting and keeping your consumers. Your business must be the first place consumers think of when they have a problem they need to solve.

Cultivate a following. Consider the specialist wine shop, for example. This level of category expert cultivates a market of Me's that's so narrow, it needs to build long-lasting relationships with its dedicated oenophiles. The experts' knowledge of what they are selling must be so on point that their Me's would not even think of going to anyone else. Build that foundation of trust that you know your stuff, and the Me's will keep coming back.

The foundation of trust in your expertise will allow you to expand. Never dilute that front line of knowledgeable associates. And if you can't offer the same depth of expertise as an REI rock-climbing expert or a Murray's cheese monger or a Madame Paulette stain remover, you must be prepared to introduce more Cs into your recipe with the same level of thought and care.

Your cart total: *Category Expert!*

Proceed to next chapter . . .

7

CUSTOMIZATION: THAT MADE-FOR-ME FEELING

The only person who acts sensibly is my tailor. . . .
He takes my measure anew every time he sees me.

—GEORGE BERNARD SHAW

When I was in business school, some enterprising tailors from Hong Kong mailed flyers to the MBA students offering deep discounts on custom suits. They set up shop in our student center loaded down with fabric swatches, took measurements, and discussed our personal preferences for how our first bespoke suit would look and feel, all at a deep discount to their standard pricing. It was smart marketing, because these enterprising artisans knew that there was a good chance many of these students would end up with high-paying corporate, consulting, or investment-banking jobs. The tailors hoped that this experience of having something made just for us would be remembered and we'd come back year after year, paying full price.

Until recently, having something custom-made was far beyond the reach of the average consumer. Savile Row, which is a small street in an exclusive area of London where the top tailors in the world have their studios, became known as the capital of men's suiting in the late nineteenth century. It's believed the term "bespoke" started with a Savile Row tailor named Henry Pool. If a customer wanted a certain fabric but it was already to be used in another gentleman's suit, Mr. Poole would inform the customer, "It be spoken for, sir." In other words, if a piece of cloth was going to be worn by Lord Nelson, the Prince of Wales, or Winston Churchill, it was for him and him only. No chance of an English aristocrat having that awkward moment at a dinner party or club luncheon. Mayfair's "golden mile of tailoring" was that exclusive. (And at upward of $10,000 a pop for a suit, it still is.)

That's the pure spirit of the *customization model* of *Me*tail, but today it can be achieved on a much larger scale. Technology has enabled average consumers to experience the feeling of having something made "just for them," even if some elements of the product are mass-produced. Consider, for example, the Nike "Shoe by You" customizer, which allows fans of the brand to choose the footwear style, fabrics, and colors they like as if they, too, are LeBron James. Advances in supply chain, manufacturing, and digital interfacing with individual consumers make it easier and more cost-effective to create the illusion of individual tailoring, even when it isn't really.

This custom segment of Nike's business now has a devoted following. Sneaker buffs have entire social media forums dedicated to speculation about when the company might make one of its more collectible shoe models available for customization. They went nuts, for example, when Nike announced that its Dunk Low sneaker, a retro silhouette that was particularly hot at the time of this writing, would be introduced on its customizing platform. Fans predicted that this model could rival the legendary Air Jordan 1, and the women's Dunk High in Varsity Purple sold out in one day.[1] It's a clever move by Nike, whose customization page reads, "Imagine your 1/1 . . . Let's make something no one has ever seen." The company closely watches what's trending among its product sales, then gins up even more enthusiasm through possibilities for personalization.

Of course, there could be a downside for some people to being so distinctive. Nike allows its customers to make their shoes so individualistic it actually helped the FBI identify one of the rioters in the January 6, 2021, Capitol Hill riots from some grainy video footage. The perp was wearing limited-edition Nike Air Max Speed Turf shoes in a color combination so unusual that it's likely only a couple of people own a pair.[2] But I digress . . .

The Age of the Memoji

Among all the Cs, customization is perhaps the most obvious model for building that relationship with your consumers. After all, we live in an age of Memojis and avatars, where there is the expectation that almost anything can be personalized. A product, whether it's a piece of jewelry, a shirt, or a shoe made just for Me, and nobody else but Me? I'll take it!

Of course, true customization is expensive, time-consuming, and highly unlikely to be deployed successfully by anyone but skilled artisans, like the shoemaker in Florence who will craft a pair of brogues for a billionaire, or the design house in Milan that makes a one-of-a-kind handbag for Oprah. But mass customization has made this made-for-me feeling accessible for a much broader audience. Nike isn't necessarily offering its Me's an infinite number of choices. But the fact that it has embedded a set number of solutions into its manufacturing line, making it capable of sewing on a yellow swoosh instead of a red one, for example, even if it's not in polka dots, still makes its customers feel as if they are making the choices. Even if it's just the illusion of bespoke, it's a powerful connection.

Customization, or at least a semblance of it, has taken hold especially in e-commerce platforms for menswear. These days, I never have to buy off the rack, because a company called J. Hilburn has all my measurements, along with my past purchases and payment details, stored in a database. The customization comes through capturing personal details of each customer, like knowing that an individual customer prefers no cuffs on his pants, or the second shirt button sewn on an inch lower to show off a tasteful amount of chest hair (as if).

One of the company's representatives, in my case a woman named Megan who you might say does the stylist equivalent of "Avon calling," comes to my home to help update my wardrobe and, possibly, my waistline measurements. By now, she knows my taste well and gives me personalized attention, then processes the orders through the company's system.

Of course, my tailor/stylist is not customization in its truest sense. This business is not making suits and shirts for me one at a time. It's simply letting me choose a particular fabric, button color, cuffs or no cuffs, and other options.

Manufacturing has advanced to the point where many apparel and footwear categories now have an array of customizing options that are both convenient and accessible. Proper Cloth's website actually reads, "You could get a dress shirt and have it tailored, but why not buy one made to measure from the comfort of your couch?" Its customization model is based on a vast array of choices, giving customers 25 different collar styles and more than 400 fabrics to browse through. But Proper Cloth's customers don't have to be left at sea, overwhelmed by so many options, because again, they have a team of stylists online for virtual consultations. That they are not, in fact, made to measure is not the point. They are made to *seem* made to measure, and that is enough to be in the customization game.

Sliding Scale

Doing business this way, which is similar in setup to Suitsupply and many others, turns out to be economical for the company because it has a relationship with a factory that's set up to manufacture small runs of product. For today's Me—the Millennials and Generation Zers who demand to be treated as individuals—this type of service and fulfillment is a plus. In 15 seconds, MTailor can do measurements on your iPhone through its scanning app. And no surprise since its founder George Zimmer also founded the old economy Men's Wearhouse, MTailor guarantees the fit "or your money back." It even claims to be 20 percent more accurate in its measurements than a human tailor.

Counterintuitively perhaps, the perfect, personalized fit doesn't cost that much more than what you'd pay going to the usual suspects for a suit because of advances in manufacturing. Mass customization through technology offers Me's clothing items that are a perfect fit when they arrive at their door, at accessible pricing.

For a friend of mine (we'll call her Candace), ordering something custom-made online turned out to be a better experience than in person. A few years ago, while on vacation on the Amalfi Coast, in a "Jackie O" moment, she decided she just had to have a pair of Capri sandals made. All the shop fronts on the street in Sorrento, where she was told all the best artisans labored, advertised the custom footwear ready in two hours or less. With just a few hours before she had to head back to the Naples airport to catch her flight home, Candace entered one of the stores, where a charming lothario helped her pick out the leather and hardware for her black-and-gold slides. Having already checked out of her hotel, she killed time doing a little more shopping and grabbing some lobster ravioli at a restaurant in a nearby piazza.

After lunch, on her way back to the sandal shop, Candace noticed row after row of shop fronts had been shuttered for their afternoon siestas, including the one belonging to the lothario. Seized with anxiety, she paced back and forth in front of the store where her sandals were supposedly being made, and for which she'd already put down a hefty deposit. Finally, the lothario craftsman returned, greeting my frantic friend with a typical Italian shrug. The sandals were finished, sort of, though they pinched slightly at the sides and there was no time to make the necessary adjustments. She's hardly worn them since.

In 2020, Candace couldn't make her annual sojourn to the region because of the pandemic. But Italy came to her in the form of shoemaker Canfora, based on the Isle of Capri. While far from high tech with iPhone scanning apps for her foot size like those of MTailor, Canfora's website did at least offer PDFs for her to print out to measure her feet almost as precisely as they would have been inside the store. Two weeks later, she was the proud owner of a glamorous pair of customized slides that fit to perfection.

"I'll go back to Sorrento anytime," Candace told me. "But more for the seafood pasta and limoncello than the footwear."

The artisans at Canfora are grandsons of Amedeo Canfora, who began selling his handcrafted sandals at a street stand in 1946; this new generation smartly leveraged technology to scale the business beyond the usual well-heeled tourist trade, attracting many more Me's, as well as press in publications like *Elle, Town & Country, Forbes,* and *O Magazine.* But for those customers still willing to make the trek to the little workshop on the Via Camerelle and have their feet expertly sized up by the able, calloused hands of Fabrizio or Costanzo, the purest bespoke experience remains an option.

Think of this C as a sliding scale between customized product and personalized experience. You can choose exactly how bespoke you wish to be. But unless you plan on charging prices that only the extremely wealthy can afford, your business model is going to need to combine some elements of mass customization and the leveraging of technology, along with details that add to the impression that the product or service is tailor-made. In the *Me*tail economy, consumers have increasingly come to expect personalization, in some form or other, in all their purchase interactions. The more special they feel, the more they're willing to pay and become repeat customers.

Bespoke Bijoux

This *feeling* of customization can come through something as small as a jewelry bar in a boutique where customers can design their own necklaces or bangles from a selection of chains and pendants. Jeweler Alex and Ani built its business around hosting parties where young girls could come in and get creative at the "Chain Station." Kendra Scott's online "Color Bar" allows customers to mix and match their own gemstones and precious metals or get charms and tags engraved. Savile Row it's not, but the entrepreneur, who started her business in 2002 out of her bedroom with just $500, figured out that balance between bespoke product and experience. Again, this new reality is Me-driven: Whether you are selling custom shirts or cruises, the customization model strikes at the heart of the largest number of Me's. Selling stuff is no longer enough if you want your Me's to feel recognized as individuals. The feeling of personalized service that goes along with the transaction is almost as important as the product itself—and sometimes even more important. Me's should always feel like something was designed with their individual needs and preferences in mind.

That Perfect Shade

In fact, with certain products, you are almost insulting a segment of Me's if you do not offer some form of customization given the technology now available. For example, take cosmetics. There was a time when the major brands manufactured in only three shades: light, medium, and dark. They didn't take into account the diversity of skin tones, particularly for Black and Brown customers. Then Rihanna came to the rescue.

A fan of makeup ever since she was a girl growing up in Barbados, the pop star recognized early on the power of makeup for self-expression. But she also saw a void in the market. As someone who spends most of her life under the stage lights, she could never find the right shade, so she set about developing a solo line of makeup with the help of luxury brand LVMH: Fenty Beauty.

This stuff was groundbreaking. Rihanna Robyn Fenty launched in 2017 with 40 shades of foundation, which was unprecedented, and product quickly sold out. In fact, the brand was named one of *Time* magazine's best inventions of that year. Fenty was so impactful that it immediately put pressure on all the other makeup houses to become more diverse.

Today, at least 30 shades have become the norm, and not just at high-service, curated stores like Sephora, where Mac, Clinique,

Lancôme, and Cover FX now have 35 to 40 shades. Even drugstore brands like Maybelline's FIT Me foundation line offers 40 skin tones, with a virtual shade finder to help customers find the closest match. Even Boots Number 7 brand has come up with a way for consumers to customize for themselves, selling bottles of foundation drops they can add to their favorite moisturizers—of any brand—allowing them to control the coverage and the intensity of the pigment.

Rihanna didn't approach her business like a traditional retailer. Instead, she looked at the market with fresh eyes and an intimate understanding of what she and a vast network of friends and fans were experiencing: a sense of being overlooked. She thought hard about her Me's, focusing on a broad range of traditionally hard-to-match skin colors and creating formulas that would work with all skin types and give consumers a range of options.

Customers can then go onto Fenty's website to use its virtual color finder to identify their undertone, then narrow it down by their shade range (light, medium, tan, deep). That's still a lot of colors to choose from, so if the online tutorial with photographs and diagrams doesn't get them to their exact, perfect tint, Fenty's Me's can book a virtual consultation with one of the company's beauty advisors. The system also points Fenty customers toward a range of lipsticks and other cosmetics in shades that complement their skin's natural color and undertones—a smart upselling strategy that gives them a customized look from the neck up.

"We got you," the Fenty site assures its Me's.

When she developed her brand, Rihanna took into consideration not only the skin pigment of her Me's, but their culture and attitudes, developing formulas that would allow them to build coverage if they chose, or keep it light, to even out their skin tone while still allowing their natural beauty (freckles and all) to shine through and "make skin look like skin." It was a timely move away from beauty conformity. Rihanna was speaking directly to her Me's when she said on the her company's website, "Makeup is there for you to have fun with, it should never feel like pressure. It should never feel like a uniform. Feel free to take chances, and take risks, and dare to do something new or different." By 2020, this strategy had been largely responsible for landing the "celebreneur" on *Forbes*'s list of richest self-made women (more so than her album sales).

While you could say that having 40 shades, or even 400, is not customization, you would miss the point. It was enough for each Me to have that chosen-for-me feeling. And that's the point. Customized does not have to mean literally made one at a time.

Signature Scent

Some beauty companies, such as the perfumier Olfactory NYC, are taking it a step further by empowering their customers to create their own signature scents. For less than $100, you can order custom fragrances online after trying out the company's nine scents from an "explorer box" that arrives in the mail. Once you've figured out your favorite, you get a "tinkerer box" to play around with, making your own blends with complementary scents that you add to the core fragrance. Then, when you've come up with your own signature smell, you can order a full bottle of your custom perfume. These are no cheap drugstore fragrances. The company, which has its original brick-and-mortar studio in New York's fashionable SoHo district, uses master perfumers from top fragrance houses to create the core scents.

Having a signature perfume was once a privilege extended only to royalty or celebrities. The great perfumiers of Europe, dating back to the days of Louis XIV, were beyond elitist about who could wear their combinations of rare oils and extracts. But now we're all entitled to the luxury of spritzing ourselves with our own blends. The same goes for custom-made lipsticks from BITE Beauty, which has Lip Labs where consumers can dabble with all the different pigments and come up with their perfect color, finish, and "flavor," with the guidance of a nearby makeup artist if they so choose. They even get to name their shade and have it engraved on the lipstick casing. It's the kind of personalized product and service that keeps the company's Me's coming back for more.

The beauty industry lends itself perfectly to these custom jobs, whether they are digital companies or not, leveraging technology, quizzes, or algorithms to customize shampoos and conditioners (like Function of Beauty) or customize skin serums and facial oils that take into account personal details like age, genetics, and specific skin symptoms (like Skin ID).

Kiehl's was already a successful high-end skin-care company when it introduced its Apothecary Preparations counters in its brick-and-mortar stores: At these counters, Kiehl's consumers can get both personalized service and products through a skin-care guru who discusses their unique concerns, asks a series of questions, and tests their skin's moisture level with a special machine. The store expert then drills down further with an analysis of skin texture, sensitivity, fine lines, pore size, whatever, to identify the two main skin concerns of the Me's, mixing and matching from a selection of what Kiehl's calls "targeted complexes," which the expert whips up in the back room. The product has a personalized label that looks as if it were typed up on a vintage Corona typewriter.

The common thread among all these custom or custom-*ish* experiences is that no detail has been spared to make the Me's feel like the product is just for them, even if there is only a finite number of formulations from which to choose.

The trick is getting the balance right between investment and the costs you are able to pass on to the consumer. It's enough that your Me's can determine some—not necessarily all—of the elements of the product or experience for themselves. And the more you can create that illusion of bespoke with small, affordable details, for example, or customizing technology that more than pays for itself, the more scalable your model.

Custom Cruising

The customization model works for more than just beauty and apparel.

Until recently, travel packages were nothing if not cookie cutter. If you wanted to go on safari in Botswana, you bought a package. Even the most luxurious of cruise liners would require choosing from among only a handful of mass excursions. Anyone who's ever vacationed in a port town in the Caribbean or Southern Europe has seen them: hundreds of dazed cruise passengers shuffling off the gangway, trying to find their land legs and their tour guides, who shepherd them onto the bus for the next six to eight hours.

But the travel industry has gotten the personalization memo. For those Me's with more to spend, there are high-end cruise line companies like Regent Seven Seas Cruises that allow passengers to design their own menus based on food favorites or dietary needs, and customize onshore excursions including personal drivers and guides. While your fellow cruisers are led through a lace factory and badgered to buy some doilies so the local guide can make his commission, you and your spouse could be driving along the winding roads to Positano in a vintage Aston Martin, heading for a Michelin star lunch on a terrace overlooking the Tyrrhenian

Sea. While this customization option introduced complexity for the cruise operator, allowing for a customizable experience attracts people who might otherwise be put off by sameness.

Coming out of the pandemic-induced lockdowns, it's a safe bet that more Me's are going to want to travel without the crowds, among friends and family from the same "bubble," so those with means might also turn to Art in Voyage, a digital team of travel "concierges" who will help their Me's design their own travel experiences, whether that's a private cruise in Polynesia with your closest friends or a biking trip through Patagonia. These bespoke travel tailors can suggest certain experiences based on input from their guests—for example, a vineyard and château stay for a group of wine and food lovers—or help them shape their own escape.

An increasing number of small-ship cruises have come online as cruisers reject the all-inclusive and crowded experience of cruise ships the size of city blocks. These boats can access passages of the Caribbean where humongous vessels can't possibly go, offering an elevated level of concierge service, with stops at "intimate" (read "exclusive") ports for champagne-and-caviar beach parties. These "boutique" ships have the staff and resources to make passengers feel so individually catered to because, in the case of the SeaDream yacht line, they have a crew-to-passenger ratio of nearly 1:1. Truly bespoke travel experiences like this aren't necessarily within reach of most Me's, but the rest of us still want to feel special, as though our trip has been chosen just for Me. Cruise lines, hotels, and airlines are scrambling to bring consumers variants of this kind of personalized service, whether it's biometric check-ins and check-outs, voice-activated room controls, or virtual concierges. Or Delta Airlines's tool for the cabin crew, which enables the crew members to access information about their most frequent flyers so that they can approach them where they are seated and greet them by name.

"Consumers are getting accustomed to a level of personalized service . . . that we have to stay competitive with," Princess Cruises president Jan Swartz told *Travel Weekly*. Personalizing every inter-action through technology "is going to drive greater and greater conversion to cruise as a vacation alternative."[3]

A More-Inclusive Middle Ground

For more mainstream companies with infrastructure already in place, the key is to rethink what it means to approach the custom-ization C. Madewell's customers are extremely loyal to the compa-ny's denim selection, among other things. Madewell offers so many styles of jeans—high, low, and mid-waist; boot cut and straight cut; and multiple colorways—that it can feel either overwhelm-ing or liberating, depending on your perspective. There are enough options in its product line to feel as though, when you find just the right one, it was custom-made just for you, even if the jeans are not exactly made for Me. American Eagle and Abercrombie & Fitch and other brands also offer this level of mass customization through a vast array of styles and sizes.

Of course, manifesting the illusion of customization requires a revolution of the basics. Most companies have spent years orient-ing their manufacturing and sourcing supply chains to chase effi-ciency versus customer centricity, but you can't have it both ways. If you are going to compete on this C, then you must go all-in, and that will likely require a different perspective on many of the metrics you're accustomed to. Consumer companies tend to mea-sure inventory "turns," for example, which is a metric of how many times they turn over (or sell) their inventory each year. More and faster somehow became the metric worth watching for many com-panies. But for the customizer, chasing inventory turns may drive you toward decisions that detract from the appearance of customization, like eliminating extra-small or extra-large sizes or removing slow-moving styles without regard for the impact on the Me's who are loyal to those particular sizes or styles.

Whatever the nature of your consumer-facing business, if you plan to compete with customization, be sure to treat your Me's as individuals. They don't want to feel like part of the herd. Give them the ability to control some aspect of their relationship with you, through either products or experience. All it takes is a little imagination and empathy for what your Me's might need and enjoy in the moment. The possibilities for creating that connection are limitless.

Even dogs and cats can get bespoke products. Well, kind of. The fresh pet-food delivery company Nom Nom uses restaurant-grade proteins and vegetables, gently cooking individual ingredients to preserve maximum nutrition, to create individual, perfectly portioned meals for pets. The customizing part comes through the at-home gut-health kit, so you can test your pet's microbiome (the microbe universe necessary for digestion, immunity, and overall health) and get feedback from Nom Nom's board-certified vet to determine which meal kits are optimal for your pet's age, breed, weight, and general health profile. If Snowball licks the bowl clean, that's a bonus.

Full confession: My wife and I use Nom Nom for our three dachshunds. My wife pampers them like children, and I sometimes think they eat better than I do, but what better business for doting pet owners—Me's—who project so much of their identity and emotions onto their animals? Our dogs can't tell us which are their favorite flavor profiles, and that's obviously not the point. It's more important that Nom Nom's human customers (who tend to also be health and environmentally conscious) feel that they are getting a customized product.

Nom Nom knows that its Me's like the fact that its growers and suppliers have been carefully vetted; that the meal prep is done in small batches, without using extrusion or high-temperature frying methods; that the meals are pre-portioned down to the last calorie; and that the food is sustainably sourced, with little to no waste. The Nom Nom team even puts the touching health stories of its customer's cats and dogs on its site, along with the names of the chefs, the person who answers the phone, and the guy who delivers the recyclable boxes to your door (Matt). Again, it's that blend of semi-customized product and service, carefully designed to project personalization, that captivates Nom Nom's pet-loving tribe of Me's. It's all about making that individual connection, by any means necessary.

Items in Your Cart

Even if it's just the illusion of bespoke, that is a powerful connection. Mass customization has made this "made-for-me feeling" accessible for everyone.

Me's don't want to feel like part of the herd. Give them the ability to control some aspect of their relationship with you, through either products or experience. All it takes is a little imagination and empathy for what your Me's might need and enjoy in the moment. The possibilities for creating that individual connection are limitless.

Mass customizing through technology may be even more appealing than old-school bespoke. It can be more convenient than visiting with a tailor in person, for example. For today's Me—the Millennials and Generation Zers who are accustomed to instant satisfaction—this speed of service and fulfillment is a plus.

Think of the customization model as a sliding scale between customized product and personalized experience. Unless you plan on charging prices that only the extremely wealthy can afford, your business model will need to combine some elements of mass customization, the leveraging of technology, and details that add to the impression that the product or service is tailor-made. The more special your Me's feel, the more they're willing to pay and become repeat customers.

Spare no detail to make Me's feel like a product is just for them. Even if there is only a finite number of formulations or models from which to choose, the technology investments, the engraver, the on-hand "expert" in person or online, allow for loyal Me's.

The customization model is well aligned with the *Me*tail economy. Selling stuff on its own is no longer enough if you want your Me's to feel recognized as individuals. The personalized attention and bespoke service that go along with the transaction are as important as the product itself. But thanks to technology, it's a wide-open field for personalization, whatever product or service category you are in.

Customization does not have to mean one at a time. It's a careful balancing act between investment and the costs you are able to pass on to the consumer. It may be enough that your Me's can determine some, not necessarily all, of the elements of the product or experience for themselves.

Your cart total: *Customization!*

Proceed to next chapter . . .

8

CURATION: THAT CHOSEN-FOR-ME FEELING

My company is an extension of me, so when I designed my stores,
I wanted people to feel that they were in my home.

—TORY BURCH, FOUNDER AND CREATIVE DIRECTOR OF TORY BURCH

While I was finishing graduate school, my wife and I had to budget carefully to make ends meet. But, of course, that didn't stop us from window-shopping. One of our favorite things to do was walk around the streets of Boston and gaze at all the gorgeous merchandise displayed in the stores' windows.

Our anniversary was just a few days away, and my wife wanted to go shopping for an outfit for our dinner celebration. There was one store in particular that she was drawn to—Tess, a small, clothing and accessories boutique on Brattle Street in Cambridge that had a selection of fashions that seemed hand-picked just for her. The store is eponymous, and the proprietor, Tess Enright, has exquisite taste and sources a selection of women's suits, dresses, shirts, and accessories that you can find nowhere else unless you have the time and resources to scour the world yourself. She spotted an emerald-green tunic and matching pants that cost more than our monthly rent, but we decided to splurge anyway. It made her so happy, and she looked gorgeous. It was one of many moments in our relationship that we still talk about and remember fondly. Better yet, she must have worn that outfit more than 20 times, so we got more than our money's worth. Sue me, but cost per use is a metric I actually think about (thanks, Dad).

As we got more established in our careers, she made a regular pilgrimage to Tess's boutique, even after we moved away. All she had to do was phone ahead to let Tess know that she was coming, and Tess would have a fitting room reserved for her for the next five hours to try on a rack full of clothes Tess had chosen just for her.

Today, my wife doesn't even have to travel to Boston. Tess ships a box of curated clothes to our home (sometimes without even telling us); she tries them on and sends back what she doesn't want to keep. This is the *curation model* of *Me*tail in the purest sense.

Curation doesn't mean unctuous service. Quite the opposite in Tess's case, because she could often be quite abrupt, but in the way your best friend or sister can be abrupt because you are on such familiar terms. On one occasion, my wife was in her fitting room, trying on some dressy jeans that Tess had selected for her. After struggling a bit, she exclaimed over the curtain, "They are too small: I can't zip it up!"

"Try harder," was Tess's response.

Tess's boutique is a bit of a mess, frankly. It is cluttered and full of racks of clothing in no particular order. There are no mannequins, no pictures on the walls, no assistants serving glasses of Prosecco to a customer about to spend a few thousand dollars on her seasonal wardrobe. Yet without Tess physically present to take he customers through each item, helping them to fit the items onto their bodies and to see the possibilities and share in her vision, her business would not be anywhere near as successful as it is.

The really special thing about Tess is that even though my wife didn't look like her typical well-heeled customer when we first went there, Tess made her feel like she belonged, and she welcomed her. Most shop owners would have sized us up on our first visit and decided we were not worth their time. But instead of being dismissive or treating us like someone who could not afford to be there, Tess recognized something in us that has paid off handsomely, for both.

It was such a stark contrast to so many other experiences where disinterested associates give the cold shoulder to people without the "right" look. It's foolish, but I am sure everyone reading this book has had a similar experience. Treating everyone with respect at first, and then curating for their customers, is how most curators become successful. They understand that they cannot live only on "current" customers and need to grow alongside their Me's.

Spending time in Tess's orbit was the same feeling we got when we celebrated our anniversaries at a restaurant called Chanterelle in the Tribeca neighborhood of New York City in the early 1990s. Chanterelle was one of the finest restaurants in the country, serving up sublime cuisine in an elegant yet intimate setting. The place had maybe 10 tables. We had to book months in advance and had to start saving that far ahead in order to be able to spend more than we should on the prix fixe menu, but it was so worth it, and not just for the melt-in-your-mouth paper-thin slices of salmon carpaccio. It was the way the owners, a married couple named Karen and David Waltuck, along with their exquisitely trained staff, made us feel: like royalty. Everything was so clearly handpicked, curated, by the Waltucks, from the menu to the decor, even the seasonal menus featuring art from art legends and friends. We still have the menu they presented us after one of our special anniversary dinners.

This is the place you tell all your friends about, not even really because of the food, which was spectacular, but because of that feeling that your meal, and in fact your entire experience, was curated for you alone. You never felt like cattle or sensed that the staff were trying to turn over the tables to get the next possibly bigger-spending party seated. Giving you the time and space to sit there and savor was the goal. The waiters never hovered, but they magically appeared just exactly when we needed something, whether it was to refill our wineglasses or replace a dessert spoon. It was as if they could read our minds. They welcomed us like regulars from our first visit, when we could barely afford to pay our bill, and we went back every year until they closed, unfortunately, when the Great Recession hit in 2009.

Consumer Concierge

You cannot fake that level of curation—choosing the products and the service levels and managing them intensely—and technology can't replace it. Customers see past the "If you bought this, you might like that" algorithms. This kind of digital customer interface doesn't replace intimate knowledge of likes and dislikes. Similarly, digital personalization (which is the latest buzzword as I write this book) is nothing of the sort. It's simply a more sophisticated way to serve up content based on past purchase behavior. But as we've already established, that bread-crumb trail is a dead end in the world of the quantum consumer. You don't ever truly know your Me's by their clicks. Using historical purchase patterns to guess a consumer's next move is like driving while looking in the rearview mirror. A true curator is someone who looks toward the horizon and anticipates your future wants *with* you.

Curation is the *Me*tail model most companies think they already have mastered, but in fact have not and never will. To be viewed in the eyes of the consumer as a curator implies that you are offering something truly differentiated. A lifestyle such that consumers don't even realize they are buying stuff. The combination of products for sale and the environment in which they are sold must elicit a truly intimate feeling. The actual purchase stems naturally from the sense that things were "chosen for Me."

Think of the ideal curator as the concierge at a luxury boutique hotel in one of your favorite destinations, say, Paris. That concierge has paid such close attention to you and your family's needs and desires, it's as if she knows you better than you know yourself. She has you booked at a new restaurant she is confident you'd like to try, and she's right. She's scoured a neighborhood you've yet to discover to recommend a jewelry boutique for your daughter to check out, and she suggests a local streetwear shop for your son. Knowing your wife's taste for Impressionist art, she's also listed a couple of museum exhibits she might like to see. She's all about anticipating your expectations and getting you to experience things just enough beyond your usual limitations to give you a sense of excitement and discovery along with comfort. Again, you cannot manufacture that kind of intimate knowledge. It feels personal because it is.

Curation does not necessarily mean fawning customer service, as we saw with Tess. As discussed earlier, customer service is a tactic, not a strategy. If it works for your business, great, but it does not rise to the level of a C, because without a C, it is perhaps necessary but certainly not sufficient. You've probably already worked out the fact that Tess does not waste a moment pandering to her clothing shop customers. To continue the hotel analogy, she would be the John Cleese character in *Fawlty Towers* to your perfect concierge in Paris (not that it would be her intention to get you to check out early). Rather, Tess will drop a pile of clothes on the fitting-room floor and order you not to come out until you've tried on every single item—and she'll know if you did not. The customer is not always right in her store. Tess is.

As is the case with the category expert, the challenge for Tess and other curators is how to scale. Because Tess is the proprietor of a small boutique, the Me's are buying into Tess as a person. These Me's are investing in her knowledge, taste, and ability to build her vision around their wants and needs. They're also trusting her to elevate their expectations, pushing her clients just enough to try out new looks or explore an aesthetic they may not have considered for themselves without her influence.

So if you want to be a curation force of nature like Tess, there is a place for you in *Me*tail, as long as you keep the business contained and under your complete control, giving every Me who walks into your store your up-close, personal, and undivided attention. Tess learned this lesson the hard way, opening and then unfortunately closing two more locations that simply could not scale; each store needed Tess herself, and even in a quantum world, that is (at the moment, anyway) impossible.

The House That Ralph Built

So if you aspire to grow as a curator, then the curation experience cannot rely on only one person. Not that curation-led expansion isn't possible; it's just incredibly tough beyond a certain point. But for those of you with growth aspirations, you need only look at the house that Ralph Lauren built, perhaps the purest example of a curator at scale that's ever existed. Somehow, he was able to curate a lifestyle for millions who never set foot on a polo field; yet they desired to surround themselves with clothing, accessories, and homeware items that reflected that sensibility—to the point where they even hung the designer's wallpaper in their homes.

So much of his personal passion and aesthetic is imbued in every detail of his stores that even though he is not physically present, no one would be surprised to see him emerging from the storeroom and giving customers a friendly nod as they browse a highly curated selection of Purple Label slim-fit blazers. Also, he had this genius way of making his brand feel both accessible and exclusive all at once. Growing up, many of my buddies would save up from their summer jobs cutting grass or grilling burgers to splurge on a Polo shirt. We may not have come from money or ever set foot in a country club except to caddy, but that little embroidered polo player and pony made us feel part of something special.

Ralph Lauren represents many things to fashion retail, but it's the way he transformed his designer clothing label into the ultimate luxury American lifestyle brand that was the envy of countless companies.

To be clear, curation does not have to be only about product; in fact, it seldom is. Companies can curate through experience, design, location, even the characteristics of the staff they hire (without violating any laws or norms). There are multiple ways even the largest brands can curate. Nike, for example, does it through a kind of hyper-localization. Its Melrose Place store in Los Angeles, which opened in 2018, provides a localized assortment of footwear and apparel, creating a mix that is exclusive to that location.

The store refreshes its collections weekly, basing its decisions on feedback from loyal customers and taking into account local conditions, such as the weather, team sports attendance, and the customer profile based on ethnicity, sociodemographics, and sizing. It does "macro and micro" space planning, organizing visual merchandizing according to this data. It's all about getting the right assortment of product in the right place at the right time and in the right proportion, so that the Me's experience Nike as less of a behemoth brand and more of a neighborhood store.

Scaling this level of carefully curated experience and product is challenging but not impossible, as Ralph Lauren and Phil Knight (the Nike founder) have proved. In fact, Nike once again demonstrates the elasticity of the Cs and how they can work together by the way it has simultaneously managed to pull off being a global mass producer of footwear while also curating some of the most passionately sought-after and hard-to-obtain sneakers on the market. The scarcity of its limited-edition shoes helps create an "aura of cool" around the rest of Nike's product lines. When Nike observes that a shoe is hot in those back channels, it carefully ramps up production, but never too much, because the company knows it's a careful balancing act between curation and market saturation, or "chosen for Me" versus chosen for everybody.

Visual Aids

Another technique for this C that enables a degree of scale is the curated experience in the form of visual merchandizing at the highest level. Dallas-based Forty Five Ten does this especially well, with an approach that is the exact opposite of Tess the purist's. Instead of "picking a lane" (in Tess's case, contemporary women's apparel), Forty Five Ten stores mix cutting-edge fashion for men and women with art and houseware items, including vintage, that you cannot buy anywhere else. In fact, walking into Forty Five Ten is like walking into a gallery of thoughtfully laid-out exhibitions that raise lifestyle to the level of art. The entire store is curated in a way that presents products to people in an environment that's five-sense–oriented. You don't need anyone to guide you when you walk through its doors. You are just drawn to a pair of hand-painted Converse high-tops on display like a piece of avant-garde sculpture. You simply must buy them.

I am curious to see how that level of curation can be sustained. How many locations in the curation model are too many? Two? Three? Or Ralph?

With the curation model, there is always the risk in chasing growth that the company will drift away from who it is as a curator. In fact, with today's Me's, choosing this particular C almost guarantees that a company will never be bigger than a certain size. Even Ralph Lauren had to suffer the ignominy of shuttering his flagship Fifth Avenue store because he chose growth for growth's sake.

Many others—including Marc Jacobs, Michael Kors, even all the way back to Pierre Cardin—have done the same by over-extending their brands in search of volume, and some (such as Ralph Lauren and Coach) are making the hard choices to get back to their roots as curators. Companies using the curation model can still have a profitable business with Me's willing to pay a premium for what they can provide them, as long as the companies don't grow faster than their ability to curate. Or if you do elect to chase sales, be sure to do it knowingly and de-emphasize the curation C in favor of another, or a combination of others. Recipes can change, but you'll never get the same dish with different ingredients, so it's important to be intentional.

Curate a Story Line

Curation doesn't necessarily have to happen in a physical store. Whatever your category and whichever platform you sell from, it's about engaging your Me's with a story in which they can see themselves. Consider the online company Huckberry, which created the "Instant Surf Shack" for Father's Day: an assortment of curated items ranging from a surfboard coffee table to high-performance Teva sandals, summer shirts, and backyard barbecue essentials. This was an ingenious way of helping their customers—their Me's—to tap into their imaginations and allowing them to think of themselves as the chiseled and tanned beach idols they wish they might become. This experience was achieved without a single physical location.

However you choose to help your Me's create their own narrative, it must never be a cookie-cutter approach. Homogenization does not belong anywhere near this *Me*tail model. Again, the point of curation is that the Me's feel they're in a relationship with someone who knows them well, from their size and style preferences to the way they like to navigate a store. Just as you could never truly know a historical figure based solely on a set of facts about him or her, current Me data is simply an accumulation of historical facts. It says nothing about the whole person.

Restoration Hardware, or RH, the furniture store, has evolved into a kind of lifestyle curator. It's no longer just a showroom full of drawer knobs, towel hooks, and pricey sofas. At last count, the home retailer has opened 18 giant galleries, as RH refers to its stores, and it is experimenting with opening bars, restaurants, turnkey residences, and guesthouses and even offering for charter a luxury yacht, all of which would be furnished and decorated with the brand's aesthetic. In 2020, it made a $105 million investment in Aspen, Colorado, using the location to create an entire RH "ecosystem" of "products, places, services and spaces" that live up to the brand's aesthetic, according to CEO Gary Friedman. The idea is to give the brand's affluent Me's a highly curated range of products and experiences within walking distance, all against the stunning backdrop of the Rocky Mountains. RH is not only curating the experience and the products; it's curating the actual location.

Of course, RH isn't the first retail brand that has expanded into other categories, as we already know from Ralph Lauren's bars, restaurants, and coffee shops in Paris, New York, Chicago, London, Hong Kong, and Tokyo. Crate & Barrel launched The Table at Crate restaurant in 2019. Pirch, the luxury fixture and home appliance retailer, has even gone as far as allowing its Me's to take a shower or cook a meal inside its stores in order to thoroughly test its products. West Elm, Bulgari, Armani, Shinola, and Muji are among those brands that also have hotels.

Curating a lifestyle where your products play a supporting role is not for every brand, but it's a winning strategy when done right, as the brand becomes a kind of guide or, again, a concierge as consumers travel, dine, and luxuriate in your carefully curated world. That said, the more you expand your universe, the more control you must be able and willing to exert.

"It doesn't matter if it's a Guesthouse. It doesn't matter if it's a restaurant. It doesn't matter if it's a residence deal. We might have a partner from a development point of view, but we will control it. We want to own it. We want it to be ours. We want to be great at it. And it's hard to be great when you're kind of licensing out parts of your business. No one's going to care as much as you. No one's going to love it as much as you," Friedman assured RH investors when he announced that huge undertaking in Aspen.[1]

That's my biggest caveat when it comes to curation. The further you get from Tess's purist model, the more you'd better be darn sure that you have poured yourself into every aspect of the business to maintain that "chosen-just-for-me" feeling. Accept that, as a curator, you can't rely on outsourcing or partnership shortcuts (unless the partnership is brand enhancing). You can never choose the expedient option. Ever.

Table to Farm

The fast-casual food chain sweetgreen is noteworthy because it feels less like a chain and more like a charming little farm-to-table eatery you happened upon as you were wandering the neighborhood. The ethos-oriented company reminds me of an episode of *Portlandia*, where an uber-hipster couple at a restaurant asks about the chicken, or I should say, "a heritage-bred, woodland-raised chicken that's been fed on a diet of sheep's milk, soy, and hazelnuts," according to their straight-faced server. The couple insists on delving more deeply into the lived experience of said chicken, not only wanting to know whether it is local, but where the hazelnuts were sourced and exactly how big the area was where the chicken was able to "roam free." Instead of proceeding with the order and finally enjoying a delicious meal, they end up leaving the restaurant and heading to the chicken ranch to make sure the fowl truly had a good life before it was served up with a side of organic quinoa and kale.

Obviously the typical sweetgreen Me's are nowhere near as fantastically earnest as this satirical pair, but the chain does cater to and curate for diners who are both health-conscious and concerned about the impact of their consumption on the world.

"We believe the choices we make about what we eat, where it comes from, and how it's prepared have a direct and powerful impact on the health of individuals, communities, and the environment," the company says on its website.

So it's about not only the food and ingredients sweetgreen has selected, but the entire supply chain, including the small and medium-sized farmers, ranchers, and fishery owners who supply the proteins, fruits, and vegetables, who are listed on each store's chalkboard daily, along with such details as the temperature on the day the beets were harvested and the composition of the soil where the lettuce grew. Sweetgreen develops its menus in collaboration with its suppliers and growers, so that whatever is in season and available from farm to table dictates the dishes sweetgreen serves up each day. Sweetgreen even provides details about its sustainability and waste management efforts, so its Me's will appreciate how much has been done on their behalf to minimize the carbon footprint of that miso-roasted corn bowl they had for lunch in Miami that day.

Sweetgreen has been intentional with every detail of how the food is prepared and presented. It boasts about making everything from scratch, bringing in only whole vegetables, whole fruits, and whole grains to be seasoned, sliced, diced, and roasted, "because food tastes better when it's made fresh." But in case you don't take the company's word for it, its kitchens are open so customers can witness this process for themselves—another way sweetgreen has thought about every way in which to demonstrate proof of authenticity in its curation.

The physical space is also intended to convey that sense of localization. Each site has its own look, using building materials that have been reclaimed from existing buildings, symbolizing renewal and reuse.

"Our guests don't go to a sweetgreen, they go to *their* sweetgreen," boasts the company's website.

It's true. When you walk in, you may even assume it's the *only* sweetgreen, because every aspect of the space has been curated to feel distinctive and local. The chain seeks out buildings with notable architectural features and interesting backstories, and it displays the work of local painters, photographers, and mixed-media artists on the walls. Sweetgreen's regional design teams also play the role of art curators, displaying locally sourced pieces often inspired by the seasons, sweetgreen's food philosophy, or features of that particular neighborhood. The company is embedding uniqueness, but it is scaling.

With all the other fast-casual healthy dining chains popping up, such as Pura Vida and Dirt, and with the challenges so many food places have faced during the pandemic, sweetgreen had to go the extra mile to create that "chosen-for-me" feeling. To that end, in September 2020, sweetgreen announced a collection of curated menus on its digital platform. After conducting research with its Me's, sweetgreen realized that at least a quarter of them like to order dishes similar to what they had before but would still be willing to try something new through the seasonal menus. The Collections menus give tailored suggestions based on individual preferences, whether based on dietary needs, seasonal preferences, or particular flavor profiles. "A culinary playlist, if you will," explains cofounder Nicholas Jammet. Oh, and never fear, *Portlandia*, because sweetgreen worked with the American Society for the Prevention of Cruelty to Animals on its "broiler chicken welfare policy."

The Jet Set

To say my next example is less concerned about minimizing its carbon footprint would be an understatement. Probably the only thing sweetgreen has in common with the Uber of air travel, Blade, is a compulsive attention to detail. The company makes hopping over to the Hamptons from Manhattan by private helicopter, or doing a quick getaway via seaplane to Nantucket, or slipping out of town for a weekend in Miami or Palm Beach via private jet, almost affordable through crowdsourcing. It finds passengers willing to pay three or four times the price of a business-class commercial airline ticket—not the typical billionaires or multimillionaires who travel this way, but consumers of means who want that next-level convenience and feeling of being part of the jet set.

But the sense of curation doesn't come only from the intense satisfaction of flying to the Hamptons over Friday afternoon traffic on the Long Island Expressway. It's the whole journey, starting with the lounges, which are intended to evoke a bygone era of aviation. The lounges are decorated in a retro mid-century style, with frayed copies of vintage editions of magazines like *Playboy* displayed on a coffee table next to dishes of warm nuts. The lounge staff and flight attendants wear custom-designed uniforms inspired by the fashions of the 1960s and 1970s. The whole highly curated experience—from the color-coded wristbands to make sure customers are shepherded onto the right flight, to the cool club music that plays in the background—makes Blade's customers feel like they've been ushered past the velvet rope of an exclusive nightclub.

Blade cofounder and CEO Rob Wiesenthal, who waxes nostalgic about getting dressed up to go on a plane as a child, back when air travel was something special, wanted to re-create this feeling for his customers through curation.

No detail is too small. Blade's Me's are invited to come up to the bar for a preflight cocktail, and most opt for a rosé served in a sleek glass sippy cup, specially designed so that there's no spillage during liftoff.

"When we first launched Blade, we weren't sure about the availability of helicopters from our operators," Wiesenthal told a *Business Insider* reporter as business was taking off. "To protect ourselves from delays, and to keep down the nerves of our customers, we started serving rosé."[2]

For Blade, the curated experience *is* the product. More companies have figured out ride-sharing technology at this level, so to keep and grow their Me's, the intense attention paid to details that create and sustain that special feeling must continue. They must never stop engaging all the senses of their customers.

Once you make this decision to curate in your consumer-facing business, if that's the path you choose, don't even think about cutting corners. Understand what you are signing up for, especially as you scale. Be ruthless about your aesthetic.

Too many companies have a bad quarter and cut their visual merchandising budget, or skip that one buying trip, or reduce the size and quality of catalogs that used to be art themselves. So many other efficiency-over-effort choices that may seem small and unrelated strike at the heart of the true curator. All those details that make the experience special are usually more expensive than the alternatives. Stick to the commitment you have made to your Me's and what attracts them to you everywhere they go, and find ways to pay for it.

I put this chapter toward the end of the book for a reason: Curation is perhaps the most difficult of the Cs to pull off because of the challenges to control what happens. For instance, if your approach is to curate an experience, you don't necessarily have complete control, because each customer will engage in his or her own way. Your Me's will determine how they feel about the experience, not the other way around. And plenty can go wrong. A failure risks tarnishing the brand in the mind of the consumer, who could start to see everything else you are selling as somehow subpar. In the curation model, there are multiple failure points along the way. Obsession about the details—every detail—is critical.

Control Freaks

The further away you get from the original source of the curation, the greater the chance there is for error. That's why, Ralph Lauren obsessed over every single detail of every store, and he embedded his aesthetic and attitude into every single person who worked for him. It's also why Chanel refuses to sell through traditional wholesale distribution channels. At the few retail partners where Chanel allows its products to be sold, it controls everything from assortment to staffing, like a store within a store. The luxe brand controls the merchandising, lighting, design, associates—everything about its brand.

In order to actualize and scale this particular C, you must brace yourself to spend far more than, say, a cost or convenience *Me*tailer, on selecting retail partners, building out stores, and curating an eco-system. Then you must continue to maintain full control, which is why this particular model is only for the strongest brands.

Even more difficult is to be a digital-only curator reaching your Me's through digital distribution. The hope is that the imagery and editorial content you produce will resonate with your customer, and it must. But the disadvantage is that you can never have the same intimacy with your Me's that you might in a physical environment. In fact, in the purest sense, a curator can actually get away with being somewhat behind the times. Tess, for example, doesn't even have a website. She takes pictures of her new collections on her phone and texts them to her customers.

As a curator, one of your greatest talents is a sense of proportion. Sure, you may be tempted to scale quickly at the first flush of success. However, just as Tess understands exactly when enough is enough as she helps my wife accessorize an outfit (keeping the shoes simple, taking away a bracelet here, a necklace there—avoiding excess always), the greatest curators are masters at balancing growth with control. They know that less is more.

Items in Your Cart

Grow alongside your Me's. Don't try to outrun your Me's. And don't allow any snobbery or lack of welcoming into your business, or you will never have a base of Me's who will grow along with you. Treating everyone with respect at first, and then curating for their customers, is how most curators become successful.

You cannot fake curation, and technology can't replace it. Customers see past the "If you bought this, you might like that" algorithms. Using historical purchase patterns to guess a consumer's next move is like driving while looking in the rearview mirror. Curators look toward the horizon and anticipate the future wants of their Me's.

True curation is tough to scale because it relies so much on the individual. Your Me's are investing in your knowledge, taste, and ability to build your vision around their wants and needs. They're also trusting you to elevate their expectations, pushing them just enough to try out new looks or explore an aesthetic they may not have considered for themselves without your influence. Scale is possible, but the curator must find a way to imbue everyone in the company with the same magic.

So if you do try to scale, be a control freak. The further away you get from the original source of the curation, the greater the chance there is for error. Maintain relentless control, and never grow faster than your ability to curate associates and employees who obsess the same as you.

Curation cannot be cookie cutter. Homogenization doesn't belong anywhere near this *Me*tail model. The whole point is that customers feel they're in a relationship with someone who knows them well. Put simply, Me's must be so blown away by the experience created by the curation that they wish to incorporate it into their own lives.

Never cut corners. The intense attention paid to details that create and sustain that special feeling must continue. Never stop engaging all five senses of your customer. The curated experience can help reinforce whatever product or service your company is selling, but never abdicate your role as curator. It's far too easy to violate the curation compact.

Your cart total: *Curation!*

Proceed to next chapter . . .

9

COMMUNITY: MAKE ME FEEL WELCOME

I refuse to join any club that would have me as a member.

—GROUCHO MARX

nless you happen to be a Goth, love punk music, or are into cult-movie merchandise, you probably haven't heard of the US mall-based retail chain Hot Topic. The stores are aimed at teens and young adults who see themselves as "counterculture," selling them everything from licensed band T-shirts and skinny jeans to Funko Pop vinyl action figures and other fringe collectibles.

Whatever the counterculture kids are into these days, Hot Topic is where they go to find it.

Beyond just being a store, wherever it opens its doors, Hot Topic strives to create a kind of community for young people, with a vibrant social media presence and a seeming ability to pivot its offerings to the next trend or obsession among its newest crop of Me's as the previous generation ages out. If you are part of this community, you feel welcome and will hang out for hours, getting to know the store staff, meeting people with the same fan obsessions, browsing merchandise you can't find anywhere else in the mall, and feeling part of a worldwide community that likes the things you like, which people in your hometown typically don't understand or care about.

The kids who frequent these stores most likely don't know it, but Hot Topic is an example of the *community model* in *Me*tail. This particular C offers companies the most flexibility, but it is also the most difficult of the six *Me*tail models to maintain over time.

Of course, I realize that the highly individual nature of Me-dom seems like it's in juxtaposition against the very concept of community. How can our quantum selves, with unique qualities as varied and infinite as the crystalline latticework of a snowflake, possibly be identified with any group? But there is no cognitive dissonance here. There will always be a natural desire for Me's to find like-minded individuals. It's human nature.

SoulPsychos

Do not fall into the trap of thinking that the community model is about segmentation or demographics. That's a fool's errand in the *Me*tail world. These consumers will continue to move like agitated electrons when you try to pin them down or put them into a customer segment. Rather, these Me's—at a particular point in time, from a wide variety of backgrounds, for a wide variety of reasons—find themselves drawn to a brand, a look, a spirit, a location, an ethos, or something even more difficult to describe. But the true root of this C is that individuals are drawn to a sense of belonging to something, whatever that may be. The community *Me*tailer is putting into the marketplace a product, service, and experience that together create a feeling of being part of something that matters to its set of Me's, whether that is sustainability through companies that upcycle gently used clothing or the zealous members of SoulCycle (whom I refer to as "SoulPsychos"), where stationary biking with a slight spiritual twist seems to be just the ticket.

Yet it's a fine line between a community and a random bunch of people who have an affinity for a particular brand. Take sneakers, for example. Nike and Adidas have legions of loyal Me's: people who just prefer a brand's shoes for a particular look or fit. But loyalty to the brand is not the point. There are also true sneakerheads who live and breathe collectible sneaks with entire closets, even storage units, full of every flavor of special kicks, just as there are wine buffs who have cellars at home and speak the same language of woody notes and berry finishes. These Me's are drawn to companies that follow the community model not only because of these companies' products but also because of these companies' passion and commitment to something that *surrounds* their products—whether that "something" is an idea, a value, a lifestyle, or a particular emotion. But if you look closely, belonging to the community is often the only thing the Me's in this model have in common.

An example of a company that focuses on community is WW International, Inc., formally known as Weight Watchers. Sure, it sells services and products, but ever since Jean Nidetch, a housewife from Queens, New York, first conceived of it in 1963, the company's purpose has been to provide members with a support group (which was, initially, six overweight friends). Today, there are more than 4.6 million members of all genders and backgrounds from all over the world, but the principle of mutual encouragement and accountability is the same.

WW changed its branding to reflect its broader, less-restrictive approach to health and wellness, and it shifted its points system to something called WW Freestyle, allowing its Me's more discretion as they save up unused points throughout the week. But it also invested heavily in its digital platform called Connect, enabling its Me's to form micro support groups with each other, but these smaller groups are all under the broader community umbrella first. WW, which is subscription-based, faced some headwinds in recent years from free weight-loss apps, but it has built such a strong community, with adaptable services and products revolving around the individual lifestyles of its Me's, that, at the time of writing, its digital community has been gaining traction.

"By delivering an engaging, holistic member experience through an innovative digital platform, we drove membership growth, maintained all-time high member retention, expanded our e-commerce presence and capabilities, and reinforced WW's position as a tech-enabled, human-centric weight loss and wellness leader," said CEO Mindy Grossman on an earnings call in February 2020.

In other words, building on that solid foundation of the community model helped the business fight through the headwinds of technology startup competition and a global pandemic. The startups may have had venture capital money to burn, but they did not have community capital.

Downward Dogs

The community model is especially active in the health and wellness industry, including companies that cater to Me's focused on exercise and self-care, like the athleisure wear company Lululemon Athletica. The company was founded in Vancouver, Canada, in 1998 as a design studio by day and a yoga studio by night. Since then, the majority of Lululemon's nearly 500 stores worldwide have been built around some kind of exercise location, be it a yoga studio or a high-end gym.

The stores have attracted a community of health and wellness believers through physical proximity. Initially, those Me's were yogis, but the sportswear retailer has since been able to expand into other product categories, such as hoodies, sweats, shorts, and other activewear, not only for its core female consumers but also for men. Lulu has carefully expanded beyond the core yoga community into a broader fitness community that includes running, cycling, and physical training, demonstrating effectively how a company can stay true to the core elements of its original community and expand to bring other, like-minded communities into the broader whole. And, if done intentionally and carefully, can be expanded wider than many companies think. For example, my daughter is a ballerina and wishes Lululemon would make leotards and other ballet gear, which (if anyone at Lulu is reading this) I can promise would be a runaway bestselling division. Lululemon has also expanded into accessories, self-care, and (through its acquisition of Mirror) a remote-teaching and workout device that looks like a wall mirror in your home when it's not in use. So the brand has brought interactive technology right into the homes of its Me's.

And that's the whole point. The community model must start with a laser focus on building that community and then maintain the honesty and integrity of the core community as it expands. But that focus doesn't mean companies pursuing this model should remain static. Just because you are known for a particular thing, it shouldn't pigeonhole you. Just remember to grow in a thoughtful way that doesn't lose touch with the very thing that attracted your Me's to you in the first place. Lulu's community wasn't only people who practiced yoga; it was the ethos that those people bring to their lives, and it turns out lots of other categories of health and wellness Me's are out there. Through both careful expansion and adherence to the ethos of its core, Lululemon was able to grow into one of the largest and most powerful global sportswear brands in the world, and its story is far from over.

As Lululemon states on its website:

> Our vision for our store was to create more than a place where people could get gear to sweat in, we wanted to create a community hub where people could learn and discuss the physical aspects of healthy living, mindfulness, and living a life of possibility. It was also important for us to create real relationships with our guests and understand what they were passionate about, how they liked to sweat and help them celebrate their goals.

I wrote about sweetgreen in Chapter 8. Even though it is essentially just an eat-in/take-out chain, the company sees itself as "building a community of people who support real food." No detail has been overlooked or spared to create a sense that the health-conscious, environmentally concerned foodie belongs. It's as if the three business school buddies who founded sweetgreen in 2007 imagined and designed the place that all their like-minded friends would enjoy.

So much of our discussion about sweetgreen could have easily fit the community model as well, except sweetgreen's focus has been on curation, and the community aspect sort of followed. But the overlap is clear. If sweetgreen were to decide that part of its strategy entails adding a pinch more community, can you imagine a better first step than locating new eateries next to Lululemon stores?

Boho Bazaar

That sense of being part of something bigger doesn't have to revolve around a specific activity like yoga. What defines a *Me*tail community can be something more nebulous. For example, take Urban Outfitters, which is among the few mid-priced, specialty retailers that have thrived while many others have declined. This success is largely because of the culture it has built around its stable of brands: Anthropologie, Nuuly (a fashion rental platform), and Free People, along with Urban Outfitters itself. The Philly-based company taps into a way of being that resonates with its tribes of Me's, whether that's Anthropologie's bohemian chic or Urban Outfitter's "young and interesting vibe." As the *Business of Fashion* put it in a recent article, "While Urban brands may not define the zeitgeist, they are able to tap into it, channeling a certain attitude or spirit."[1] The company has its finger on the pulse of its community, and if it ever allows itself to stray, it will be just another retail store selling stuff. That zeitgeist is the Urban Outfitter's North Star.

Founded in 1970 by Richard "Dick" Haynes and his then wife Judy Wicks, the company's first store was The Free People, which focused on 1950s clothing, jeans, records, and vintage furniture—goods for what Dick infamously described in a September 2012 industry Analyst Day call as "the upscale homeless." The community of those first stores was made up of the free-spirited young men and women in bell-bottom pants who lived on or near college campuses, always ready to leap into the next protest march with social justice mantras written on handmade placards. Back then, buying secondhand was a kind of hippie, anti–Vietnam War rebellion against the bourgeois establishment. The stores were renamed Urban Outfitters, but that boho spirit remained, along with the cool, flea market feel of its merchandising. The first locations even felt like part of the neighborhood, benefiting from the foot traffic of like-minded consumers.

Today, the Urban ethos appeals to a broad range of tastes and sensibilities, but they are contained within a distinctive enough wheelhouse that its community of Me's can still see themselves in the hip, but not overly trendy clothing and accessories collections. Rather than dictate fashion trends (as the *Business of Fashion* case study observes), the company builds its merchandising and supply chain around what its consumers crave, closely observing their sentiments and the market to come up with a range of products, including "clean cosmetics" lines, upcycled vintage dresses, retro Polaroid-style cameras, mid-century modern turntables, and (again) vinyl records. It tests out new labels and store concepts, gathering customer feedback on social media and using its nimble supply chains to continually update and tweak to reflect changing tastes, which also means it's using another C: curation.

"It used to be that merchants would come in Monday morning and look at sales," former Anthropologie chief executive David McCreight said in an earlier interview. "Now we are coming in talking about social. It's a way for her [our customer] to speak to us or to eavesdrop and observe conversations about brands. The little insights give us the most profound advice."[2]

Where other retailers with similar origins (such as The Gap and The Limited) went the more traditional routes of mass commercial expansion, Urban's Me's can still feel like they're walking into some great neighborhood shop, whether one of its stores is in a shopping mall or in one of its many unique, historic locations like an old mansion on Philadelphia's Rittenhouse Square. Similarly, whether it's on New York's Fifth Avenue near Washington Square Park, or in Rockefeller Center in the center of Manhattan, or just off Lincoln Road in Miami Beach, Anthropologie customers feel like they've just walked into a spacious, scrubbed-pine antiques market. That sense of discovering something unique, retro, feminine, and fun inside a store that speaks to them is what bonds Urban's community of Me's.

Something Bigger Than Me

Being a community *Me*tailer doesn't have to put you in a box. There is plenty of scope for attracting your tribe, or tribes, of individual Me's. Chewy has built intense loyalty around its community of pet lovers. It goes as far as to scan customers' social media to see what is going on in their lives as pet owners. If someone's animal dies, Chewy sends a condolence letter. Chewy has a "giveback" tab on its home page that takes you to a whole list of shelters and animal rescue programs across the country that its customers can give to, with a shelter and rescue finder in their neighborhoods, where they can volunteer or donate directly.

Chewy breaks it down with individual stories of pets rescued and shelters helped with Chewy's $62 million–worth of product donations, such as the 100,000 pounds of pet supplies sent out to support the 800,000 or so federal government workers who were furloughed during the pandemic lockdown in the United States. For pet-loving Me's who are actively involved in animal causes, Chewy invites them to plug into their own network of organizations and resources, so that they can expand their own reach. There are no limits to this pet-loving identity (unless you don't like pets). Chewy could even build on it from a product standpoint and sell products like apparel and food for humans. When the community is strong enough, there are many ways to scale.

Another important binding agent for building a successful *Me*tail company based on the community model is a sense of being part of something bigger than yourself. There's nothing more effective at making Me's feel good about themselves and your brand than giving back in some way, whether through something as small as forgoing the return of an item if you donate it to a cause (the Black Rifle and Chewy examples from earlier in the book) or buying items made from sustainably sourced or upcycled material.

Otherwise known as *circular fashion*, there's a large and growing movement toward recycled retail or sustainable products that have been manufactured to have the lowest-possible impact on the environment. Companies such as Allbirds and Rothy's (which makes sneakers from recycled materials) have gained a loyal following. They're facing competition from such companies as Cariuma in Brazil, which uses only organic, fair-trade materials, whether that's rubber from natural and sustainably farmed rubber trees or leather sourced from areas that were not deforested for cattle farming. Cariuma ships shoes in the shoe box with no other packaging, to eliminate waste, and it purchases carbon offsets for shipping. Startup Nothing New makes sneakers out of recycled material exclusively and promotes recycling by offering $20 discounts on new pairs when its Me's send in their used shoes to be either cleaned and donated or broken down and used again for production material. And there are hundreds more like these.

Today's Me's—especially though not exclusively Millennials and Gen Zers—are becoming acutely aware of the havoc the fashion industry has been wreaking on the environment. Next to the oil industry, it is the largest polluter in the world due to its long supply chains and energy-intensive production methods, spewing 2.1 billion tons of global carbon emissions in 2018 alone, according to a report by *Global Fashion Agenda*.[3] It's responsible for 10 percent of greenhouse gas emissions and 20 percent of global wastewater, according to the United Nations.[4]

The amount of fabric that's wasted in factories and of discarded clothing that goes into landfills is truly staggering. Anyone who has ever stood in a Goodwill distribution center understands the need for circular fashion. Even Goodwill can't process the sheer volume of garments pouring in, much of which ends up compressed into bails and chopped into chunks, destined for rag factories.

Passion for Trashion

Enter thredUP, an online consignment and thrift store "for you, your wallet, and the planet" that has created an online community of Me's looking to buy secondhand fashion for women and children (for now, but you can be sure it will enter the men's market at some point). It's become a leading platform in a $50 billion and growing resale economy, with millions of Me's able to shop more than 45,000 different brands at prices discounted up to 90 percent. It takes the work out of sending used or unwanted clothing out for consignment (convenience). The Me's who want to make room in their closets just have to download the app and request a kit. When they fill up their bags, the San Francisco–based thredUP sends a shipping label, and when the items are quality checked, approved, and sold, the user can take either cash or a thredUP store credit.

These Me's can also choose simply to recycle their old clothes, for which thredUP donates $5 to the nonprofit Circular Fashion Fund. Meanwhile, buyers can choose anything from top designer brands in mint condition to "Rescues," for those Me's who are willing to give more damaged garments some TLC.

The company's secret sauce, the reason it's able to practice "re-commerce" with such efficiency and at such scale, is its technology. The company has invested heavily in the design of a resale engine, logistics, and infrastructure, allowing it to handle more than 100 million garments from closets across America. It uses AI to process incoming items through image recognition, enabling it to almost instantaneously tag the origin of a piece of clothing based on its pattern, label, color, and styling and assign a fair resale value based on wear and tear. ThredUP also uses technology to bring some personalization to its service, though as we discussed in the chapter on customization (Chapter 7), personalization without the physical intimacy of face-to-face interactions is just guessing. Based on past uses, predictive analytics, and trend data, thredUP's sustainable stylist handpicks 10 items for its individual members (curation) through its Goody Box service—an enhanced curation without the carbon-footprint guilt, if you will. This also allows customers to try before they buy, while enabling thredUP to get more items into customers' hands, leading to yet more sales. See how this service also happens to neatly solve a business problem for the company?

The result is that thredUP's Me's not only get to feel good about their fashion choices; they can be part of the solution to a major environmental problem, or even early adopters of a movement that seems poised to overtake fast fashion in the future as more shoppers think secondhand first.

"ThredUP intends to find a home for every item that comes in through our closet cleanout kits," the company's cofounder and chief technology officer explained to *Forbes* magazine. "Whether that is a resale to another eco-conscious or budget-inclined consumer, resale to physical thrift stores, donations to charity, or having items recycled into other textile forms, our goal is to keep those items out of landfills entirely."[5]

ThredUP also partners with major retailers, including Macy's, JCPenney, Madewell, even Walmart through its Resale-as-a-Service platform. It's a way for these retailers to participate in the sustainability trend, although it's by no means enough to turn these companies into community models for like-minded Me's looking to avoid polluting the environment. Sustainability is not a material part of the equation for most retailers, but offering their customers the option to buy secondhand is certainly a start.

Closet Full of Denim

Giving back cannot be an afterthought, especially in a *Me*tail model built around Me's who want to do right by the world. A company that brands itself as rallying behind a cause needs to feel authentic and consistent, with all that you do in the name of selling products and transacting with your community of Me's and their values. It must permeate the very DNA of your business. If not, these consumers will quickly see through it and assume you are just virtue-signaling to sell more stuff.

Levi's has been experimenting with upcycling, offering to buy back its customers' old jeans and jean jackets through Levi's SecondHand, both to give fans of the brand more options for that worn-in, vintage feel that extends the life of the products and to allow its other customers to feel good about upcycling their cast-offs while being rewarded with gift cards toward their new threads.

The buy-back system allows sellers to bring their used jeans into stores for a $15 to $25 credit for plain old denims or a $35 gift card for coveted vintage jeans. Jeans that are falling apart and can't be resold will be rewarded with a $5 credit before they're sent off for recycling. The still-wearable items, after some refurbishment, will then be made available for purchase on a microsite managed by an upcycle startup called Trove, which provides the e-commerce technology along with all the messy logistics of cleaning, processing, and packaging for resale.

As Levi's points out on its website through infographics, buying a pair of used jeans versus new helps Me's reduce their carbon footprint on the transaction by about 80 percent, or 700 grams of waste. It also points out that extending the life of clothing by an extra nine months of active use will reduce carbon, waste, and water footprints by around 20 to 30 percent per item. In the larger picture, according to Levi's research, global consumers lost about

$460 billion of value each year by throwing away still-wearable clothes.

The SecondHand platform is part of other efforts by Levi's to promote the circularity of its brand, which has turned up in vintage stores for decades. In 2020, it also launched a "sustainable" jeans line made from organic cotton and Circulose, a fabric made from recycled denim and viscose, which was invented by the Swedish recycled-textile-technology startup Re: newcell.

Although they are laudable, Levi's sustainability efforts may not necessarily go far enough to qualify the more than 160-year-old company as a community *Me*tailer just yet, but the company is clearly serious about trying. If not done carefully and consciously, changing its recipe as needed, it could seem as if Levi's is trying to latch onto the community trend as opposed to truly committing to a circular economy. Total dedication to sustainability would radically reshape Levi's as a company, but total dedication is the only way for this C to be real in the eyes of your Me's. If the company were to stop manufacturing denims today, there would still be enough jeans to dress every citizen of the world in jeans for the next several years before anyone would notice. And if that sort of total commitment were to take hold, it could put a real dent in Levi's profit. The key question for Levi's is this: How close can it get, and how can it reshape its revenue model along the way?

Just think about how many pairs of jeans you have in your own closet right now, many of which you probably haven't worn for several seasons. Multiply that number by all the other under-loved jeans in the closets of all the Me's, and you get the idea.

My point is that companies must take the time to think more deeply about what differentiates them before orienting their entire business model around it. The need to be all-in is true of all the C *Me*tail models, but community is especially tricky. It's much more than a corporate strategy or feature to try to connect with customers. When you build a community, it cannot just be about promoting your commercial interests. Of course, your model must enable you to stay in business. But if you're an outdoor retailer in a mountain town and all you do is sell products, you've missed an opportunity. You could become a place where Me's can interact with fly-fishing guides, for example. You could enhance your brand and build long-lasting loyalty by becoming a connector of like-minded Me's who love the great outdoors. You could take back old products or manage a product-swap program. There are so many ways to build a complete community around your business.

And if that's the path you choose, stick to it! If your community involves youth sports, then when the going gets tough, never ever cut the Little League sponsorship budget. Always come back to your North Star.

Team Deconstructed

Of course, a true sense of community is especially difficult for companies to maintain in a world where they must keep up with the ever-changing needs and wants of their Me joiners.

Consider the phenomenon of fantasy sports, which has created a generation of people who are more loyal to the platform their fantasy picks play on (such as FanDuel or Draft Kings) than the most rabid sports fans were to their team in decades past. We are fast approaching a future where no one cares much about my beloved Boston Red Sox or any other hometown team. These fans care about the fantasy team in the fantasy game they are playing with their friends.

Technology has made it possible for Me's to completely deconstruct every movement, every action, and every play in traditional sports. For example, NFL Next Gen microchips are embedded in football players' shoulder pads to track how fast they run or throw or how high they jump. Fantasy sports is just an accumulation of individual plays by individual players who are being tracked by this technology, and the disloyalty to teams results purely from the act of deconstruction that has been enabled by these digital innovations. As I write this, fans can watch multiple football games on multiple feeds to see how their individual players are performing in real time. It's not absurd to imagine a world where the outcome of a particular game doesn't even matter to the average fantasy fan. A new generation of fans may be less interested in whether the Red Sox win or lose than if their fantasy player hits a home run or strikes out.

In the distant future, you could easily imagine a world where even the slightest movement by a player is tracked and embedded into a fantasy sports or gambling platform, or both. With every player chipped and cameras from all angles tracking his or her every move, it may be eventually possible for fans to watch an amalgamation of athletes playing live in separate games at the same moment on their own fantasy app—a kind of postmodern, meta sport that is completely disconnected from the construct of team as we know it. They will be watching Player A compete against Player B in a game that does not actually exist but is a construct of their own making. The Me's will put these athletes on their own teams because it is *they* who control the narrative. Although this hasn't happened yet, it's on the horizon—something for sports-franchise executives to consider as they seek to fill up empty stadiums.

Fantasy sports is a perfect example of how the power of information is upending traditional models. Me's are using technology to strip everything down to its core elements to do with what they will. They are less loyal to a brand now because they don't have to be. Without a core C that is carefully crafted and maintained (or even with one), the brand is nothing more to your consumers than a platform through which they can obtain an item they want at a price they want through a seamless transaction.

Building and sustaining an authentic sense of community will go a long way toward holding consumers' attention. But recognize what you are up against. Boston Red Sox fans are the ultimate community model. They suffered together and commiserated with each other for 86 years. But how do you keep that going in today's world, where the lovable loser community is gone and quantum Me's are deconstructing, splintering, and re-forming in multiple locations, simultaneously, ad infinitum?

The Watercooler Experience

Whether you are a pure e-commerce platform or a brick-and-mortar store, the successful community *Me*tailer must constantly strive to find ways that allow consumers to connect. As individual as we are, we are also wired to seek things in common and share who we are with the world. Poshmark—the online secondhand retailer for men, women, and, most recently, their pets that allows subscribers to shop each other's closets—has figured out how to do this in a way that feels seamless and natural to its business model. Poshmark has created a community that is powered by millions of sellers who interact with one another. A hybrid between a social e-commerce and peer-to-peer platforms, Poshmark enables its Me's to curate looks for each other and form their own niche chat groups, for a kind of virtual-watercooler experience.

"What we are trying to do is to bring back that human connection that you have in shopping," Poshmark's CEO and founder Manish Chandra explained during a virtual seminar soon after the company's debut on Nasdaq (where it immediately doubled its offering price). "You can browse the stores as if you're in a mall or a boutique and have the conversation and discovery experience while bringing all the ease, scalability, and convenience of e-commerce."

However, that conversation is not happening in brick-and-mortar stores, which could learn from the creative way Poshmark is creating digital connections. The company has a feature on its website called Posh Stories where users can post videos, photos, and texts about their finds, in much the same way Bass Pro and REI encourage their Me's to post their fishing and hunting tales.

Once more, that is exactly what I am urging you to do in the community model: Let your Me's tell their own stories. Create a wide-open space that allows and enables them to share who they are, creating their own narratives as they weave in and out of each other's tall tales.

Items in Your Cart

It's less about the stuff you sell than the big idea that surrounds it. Me's at a particular point in time find themselves drawn to a cause, a look, a spirit, certain values . . . There is something about what the community *Me*tailer is putting out into the marketplace that creates a feeling of being part of something that matters to its set of Me's.

Don't lose touch with whatever drew your Me's to you in the first place. Building and sustaining an authentic sense of community will go a long way toward holding the attention of your Me's. But recognize what you are up against. Whether you are a pure e-commerce platform or a brick-and-mortar store, you must constantly strive to find mechanisms that allow consumers to connect in ways that feel authentic.

Just because you are known for a particular thing, you can grow. Yes, you can expand your community, if you do it in a thoughtful way that's true to your DNA. When the community is strong enough, there is plenty of scope for attracting and expanding your tribe (or tribes) of individual Me's.

Make your Me's feel a part of something bigger. There are few things more effective at making Me's feel good about themselves and your brand than giving. But a company that brands itself as rallying behind a cause needs to feel authentic, with all that you do in the name of selling products and transacting with your community of Me's and their values. It must permeate your business. If not, these consumers will quickly see through it. Community is much more than a corporate strategy or gimmick to connect with customers.

Whatever your chosen C may be, never take the loyalty of your Me's for granted. A true sense of community is especially difficult for companies to maintain because they must keep up with the ever-changing needs and wants of their Me's. So expect to work hard and smart to create a space that consistently makes your Me's feel like they belong.

Your cart total: *Community!*

Proceed to next chapter . . .

PART III

ADDITIONAL INSIGHTS

As I've introduced the *Me*tail concept to executives, I've come to anticipate the moment when the penny drops and recognition sets in. This shift is so profound that when its implications do finally land, the pit-in-the-stomach feeling is palpable.

People all have their *aha* moment and then, inevitably, start to picture the money, time, and resources they've wasted chasing the old consumer. But when I steer the conversation back to the here and now of their own businesses, I often find that executives can't quite make the leap from the abstract to what to do next. This next section is a start at helping answer that question.

10

WHAT TO DO ON MONDAY MORNING

If a problem has no solution, it may not be a problem,
but a fact—not to be solved, but to be coped with over time.
—SHIMON PERES

When people ask me the "Now what?" question after hearing this book's core premise, what they're really seeking is a framework for evolving their company into a *Me*tail player. So even though this book has been steadfastly nonprescriptive, I feel a responsibility to at least give you some kind of road map, a Monday morning to-do list, if you will, to help launch you on your way.

The pervasive disconnect I experience between executives understanding the change but struggling to link it to action suggests to me that the concept is easy enough to grasp at a high level, but like quantum physics, it's extremely difficult for most people to absorb at a visceral level, where it can transform old habits and attitudes. Overcoming muscle memory is hard. Executives become accustomed to doing things the way they always have because that is what got them into the executive suite in the first place. And let's face it, most people are risk averse by nature. But is it risky to change course if the new consumer reality I have discussed is upon us? I'd say no—it's risky *not* to.

In order to take those initial steps, the entirety of the company must be evaluated through a *Me*tail lens.

So the first thing I prescribe is to stop, think, and ask the tough questions. The *really* tough questions. Understand where you are now in relation to your consumer but with a *Me*tail lens; then allow yourself unconstrained thinking about what you might do differently if you had a magic wand. Then, because you don't, you need to do the hard work that follows.

Bear with me for a moment for an example of a thought starter rethinking of conventional wisdom that may be helpful in opening your aperture. Consider the role of the district manager. Many multiunit consumer businesses have a position called district manager or area manager or something along those lines. This is the management layer closest to the store, but not inside the store. For a 1,000-location chain, you might have one head of stores, four or more regional managers overseeing a wide geographic area, and then maybe 75 to 100 district managers with a span of oversight of 12 to 20 locations each—sometimes more.

These district managers used to play a vital role in performance management at the location level: They trained, hired, and brought best-practice know-how into the store. And they could, because, historically, the span of control (how many locations for each area manager) used to be much smaller than it is today. For years, in an effort to reduce costs, companies have been increasing the span of control of the district manager role, assuming that nothing would change. But, of course, it does, and the result is that the more locations a district manager must oversee, the less impact that manager can have on the locations they manage. At that point district managers become overpaid auditors, checking checklists and spending almost no time in stores actually helping them to improve performance, which is really the only point of the role of these managers.

But here's a secret: At most multiunit consumer companies most of the time, 80 percent of locations are doing just fine. Of the 20 percent that are underperforming, 80 percent can be attributed to underperforming store management, which is an HR issue. Another chunk has some sort of structural issue (for example, an anchor store closed in the mall, a highway was rerouted, a town lost a big employer and is in decline, etc.). Typically, there are only a small percentage of locations in a given multiunit portfolio that could and should be good stores, they have all the right elements, but are performing badly for reasons other than bad luck.

Rather than spend millions on area managers who cannot possibly spend enough time in any one location to make a difference in a model where most of the time you don't need that difference, why not create a SWAT team of sorts? This would be a small but sharp group of operatives who could spend quality time helping the stores that can be improved through better focus and execution and then moving on to the next set and the next. Then take the millions you save and invest them in your Cs.

It's one, perhaps crazy, example but the point is when you step back and see the inevitability of *Me*tail, you will discover all kinds of ways to realign your operations to save the money you'll need to reallocate in ways that are better oriented toward your Me's.

So go ahead and slaughter the sacred cows! You don't have a choice. You need to figure this out and fund it yourself. Could you get lucky and have a special-purpose acquisition company fall out of the sky and save you? Sure! But should you count on it? Well, I wouldn't. Instead, plan to find the resources necessary to enhance your strengths on your own.

Another effective way to approach your *Me*tail retrofit is to work from back to front. Start with the end in mind, your C recipe. Define your root principle of Cs; then deconstruct every aspect of your operations. Ask if an aspect supports your C. If yes, it stays. If not, it goes. If you're not sure, save it for later. It's helpful to take this approach because it is so easy to lose your way if done from current operations up, versus from the future you want, back. Stick to your C or Cs, and keep that clarity of vision as you evaluate everything you currently do. Ask why, and then ask why again.

What follows is a simple, five-stage process for sole proprietors, CEOs, and everyone in between, to help internalize what needs to happen. Call it an executive action plan (EAP).

Step 1. Forget Your Limitations

Wait, what? I thought we were supposed to acknowledge our limitations? Not in this phase. This is the discovery part of the executive action plan. Your limitations have nothing to do with your ambitions. Think deeply; brainstorm; study other models; explore all possibilities to establish your desired C recipe. By all means, take a clean sheet of paper or do a "blue-sky" whiteboard exercise, jotting down whatever comes to mind with the big, bold strokes of a chef or artist.

Ask yourself, "If money were no object and I want to manifest the glue that holds my Me's together, what is the recipe of C ingredients that I need to provide them today, tomorrow, and in the future?" While this question is naturally going to be connected to your limitations, it is important to not let them get in your way at this stage. Push yourself to go far beyond where you are now, enabling you to think about the possibilities.

Then, slowly, start to come back toward reality. Let that hot-air-balloon basket rise high enough in the air that you can see over the horizon, but keep the rope tethered to the ground. Then prepare for Step 2 where you pull yourself back to earth slowly, so you can link your ambitions to your limitations.

Step 2. Bring Back Your Limitations

Once you accept the premise of *Me*tail, you must be ruthlessly critical of yourself. You must constantly go back and remind yourself that whatever you wish to be the case, doesn't matter now. The customer has changed forever, and this has implications for your business, and hope is not a strategy.

Many executives are good at blue sky thinking, but then are unable to execute effectively against the strategy. My contention is that's largely because strategy without consideration for limitations is unattainable. The key to making real change in my view is recognizing your limitations and not wishing, hoping, or deluding yourself into thinking that you are bigger, stronger, faster, and smarter. For example, I remember the day I realized I had a better chance of owning season tickets to a professional sports team than playing for one, and as much as I wanted to play for the Boston Red Sox, I was never going to have a 95-mph fastball. We all have limitations as individuals, and so do businesses. Your company's limitations might be legacy technology, legacy locations, a legacy, or something else. And you can't fool anyone, so why fool yourself? And just like personal growth, there are no shortcuts to business growth either.

Let me tell you my favorite shortcut story. In 2014, nobody would have confused RadioShack for a high-performance retailer. Multiple misguided turnaround efforts led by the best strategy consulting firms had failed (remember The Shack rebranding effort?), and the company found itself short of cash and customers. But instead of accepting the reality and taking steps to do the unglamorous work of digging its way out of the ditch, the company decided to spend millions on a Superbowl ad. In the commercial, two sales associates are standing at the counter of an empty RadioShack store when the phone rings. One of the young men picks up, then turns to his work buddy and says, "The '80s called: they want their store back," followed by a cornucopia of hilarious 1980s references: exaggerated fade haircuts, Alf, Hulk Hogan, the Chucky doll, and even the dancing California raisins. The walking anachronisms proceed to clean out the store, and the commercial ends with the line, "It's time for a new RadioShack." Notwithstanding the fact that the ad was hilarious, it changed nothing other than further blowing the company's quickly evaporating cash on expensive 1980s celebrity cameos; a short time later, RadioShack filed for bankruptcy.

Just to drive the point home, let's say you've decided that online excellence is critical to your *Metail* journey. Fair enough. But let's also say that you are a company that's not known for digital excellence, and to make it even tougher, you're also located in a location that not known for attracting digital talent. An all-too-typical response is to acquire a digital company hoping that its DNA will somehow infect legacy teams, and we've already discussed the challenges with that approach.

Another "solution" is an attempt to hire someone with the "right" résumé, in the hope that one person can make the difference, forgetting that an entire team would need to be built behind that hire. Yet another common reaction is to open a digital center in a hot city in the belief that your location is the only thing stopping digital talent from joining you. But what it really comes down to is one simple question. Ask yourself this: "If I were a recent graduate from one of the top computer science programs in the world, where would I work?" Amazon? Facebook? Google? Or a struggling retailer with no digital excellence to be found?

True power comes from operating within boundaries, concentrating your strength where it can have the most impact, and only then expanding beyond those limits. Too many companies are obsessed with "becoming digital." They invest in the latest digital trends, spending hundreds of millions of irreplaceable dollars. If you ask them why, they will say, "Because we need to undergo a digital transformation." Ask them to define "digital transformation" and you will generally get blank stares or some mumbling about leveraging AI and big data. But if they accepted their limitations, they would realize that in order to truly stand out in today's digital ecosystem, or at least be a real player, a company needs the best minds, the best thinkers, the best practitioners.

And yet they cannot ever hope to attract that talent. There is your limitation, laid bare and probably to chilling effect. So, if where you started, that online excellence is needed for your C journey, cannot be manifested to support your C the way you had thought was required, then you *must* come up with a different approach. Realism is not fun. Nobody likes to accept the concept of "we can't," or "we can't *right now*," but trust me—you must think this way.

Just like I'll never hit 95 on the radar gun, you'll probably never recruit the Nolan Ryan of digital. Sorry to have to be the one to break it to you.

Step 3. Cost It Out

You just did the hard work of defining your C recipe. You now know in your gut that you cannot compete successfully if you do not manifest that destiny. Welcome to the real world. This phase is about determining what you *can* do to compete. There are many things more important than money if you hope to succeed as a *Me*tailer, but unfortunately, they all cost money. So you need to figure out how to pay for what you want to do.

The reason I separate the journey from the cost is that if you try to do both at the same time, or try to work out the cost first, you will talk yourself out of the best ideas and almost certainly underestimate the costs. But if you went through Steps 1 and 2 correctly, you now have your plan. It is a departure from where you were heading, but it is also grounded in your limitations and the reality of your situation. You know what you need to do, so now you can realistically assess how much it will cost.

If your organization has never implemented a technology project on time and on budget, for example, don't assume you will now. But if your *Me*tail transformation *requires* technology and you see no way around it, then budget twice the cost and time you think it will take, being realistic about the kind of talent you'll be able to attract to execute your project.

And if you have a nationwide footprint of stores and you don't need them all, realistically assess the costs of transitioning to the right footprint. Don't cut corners just because the transition looks too costly.

One warning that should be obvious but I feel compelled to remind you is to never abandon your core customer. If your *Me*tail transformation requires you to migrate to new Me's, fine, but not at the expense of your current Me's. Trust me—it will take you far longer and cost way more than you think to make the transition to a new customer, and if you ignore your core customer while you do it, you can be pretty sure that your next transformation will take place in bankruptcy court.

Finally, don't focus only on operating costs. It's highly likely that your transformation will also have an impact on your margins. For example, if you intend to expand customer-friendly policies, such as free shipping both ways for online purchases, make sure your models don't assume historical rates of margin on online purchases. Sounds simple, but you'd be shocked how often I see companies make these mistakes.

I have learned a lot as I've led companies through transformations over the course of my career. Here are two of the most paramount lessons:

- Everything takes longer and costs more than you think. It's like a home remodel: Have you ever heard anyone say, "My remodel cost half as much as I thought and took half the time?" That same thing is especially true in business transformations.
- And recall Joel's immutable law from Chapter 3: Money = Time = Options. This equation only works in one direction. Too many options can be paralyzing. But it always works this way. Find that money first and foremost, so that you can buy the time to figure out what the best options are and implement them.

If you've followed the EAP up to this point, then you have already identified your transformation and you also have a realistic assessment of the cost. This can be daunting, and may seem impossible at first. The refrain I hear in boardrooms around the world is, "There's simply no way we can afford this." But you already know the answer: You can't afford not to. Now that you know you must provide these services to the Me's, you can't turn around and say you cannot afford them. You must figure out a realistic way forward, as I outline in the following step.

Step 4. Reorient and Reprioritize

It is almost a certainty that in order to make your vision of *Me*tail happen, you will need to invest more than you think you can. But this is old thinking. New thinking will require a willingness to slay all kinds of sacred cows. For example, I don't care how many decades that store location has been a part of your business. If there's no more customer traffic, it's time to close it and put the capital you've just freed up toward things that will enhance your relationship with your Me's.

Think about ways to reprioritize, like the district manager example. This is about the creative destruction of the old ways of doing things in order to make *Me*tail happen. Think through all your costs and ask why, and why again. This part will be painful, but there is no way around it. You need to rethink every single practice, policy, procedure, and person from the lens of having to pay for your *Me*tail transformation journey.

In March 2021, we had perhaps the most ambitious example of this in retail history, when Saks Fifth Avenue announced that it was splitting its digital business into a separate company from its stores. Brilliant or nuts (I think brilliant), it allowed Saks to unlock value and raise capital at a high valuation for its faster-growing digital business. Capital it needs to reinvent itself as a *Me*tailer. Of course, Saks needs to figure out how to operate seamlessly from a customer standpoint, but that's just execution. Saks started with the end in mind, needed capital to invest, and was willing to shatter convention to go get it. And then willing to do the hard work necessary to change their operating model.

Step 5. Look Up, Often

On long journeys, course drift is inevitable. It is essential that you stick with the program. Recognize the duration of the journey, and take steps to ensure you don't lose your way. It won't be easy, and baby steps won't cut it. Many executives who commit to a strategy lose patience when their strategy doesn't start bearing fruit as fast as they'd like. They start making cuts to make the quarter, not realizing that each incremental trim is, in aggregate, stealing from the long-term vision and defeating the whole purpose of the reinvention. Do all you can to recognize those moments of self-sabotage.

Two essential ways to help are, first, to plan for regular check-ins to ensure everyone is on track and, second, to frequently communicate with your stakeholders—all of them, internal and external. Say what you are going to do and why, and then say it again and again. Get ahead of bad news, don't sugarcoat, and don't lose courage. Why? Because, remember, there is *no* alternative. If you went through Steps 1 through 4, then you already know this. So now that you've gone through all this pain and done so much of the necessary work, don't lose your nerve and don't lose your way. There is too much to be gained, or lost, depending on your perspective.

Finally, let me leave you with these general pointers as you embark on your *Me*tail turnaround:

- Act promptly, even if that means proceeding with imperfect information. Be bold and decisive, and remember, it's hard to permanently break stuff, and it's easier than you think to fix what you break.
- Remember, scrappy almost always wins. Find a way, because there almost always is one. Even if it's temporary, that's more than OK, because short-term solutions often outlast their creators.

- Trust the 80/20 rule—it works. Fast is better than perfect, whether you're doing analysis or initiating the plan. Instead of dotting every *i* and crossing every *t*, get that money coming in sooner rather than later (remember, Money = Time = Options). I sometimes frame this for clients as thinking about commas, not decimal points.
- Be direct with your stakeholders about what you are doing. Don't keep them in the dark and don't pretend something is blue when it's green. Avoid corporate-speak and just say what you mean.

> **Your cart is full: *Your Me's await!***

EPILOGUE

THAT WAS THEN, THIS IS NOW

This new consumer reality has not been well understood by most, but throughout this book, you've had your wake-up call. You have the competitive edge, because now you know and accept this crucial point that the power has inverted from the seller to the buyer. Now you understand that the power to message, the power to select, and the power to support or critique—all the things that created an uneven playing field for millennia—belong to the people.

This is exciting news, folks! We are living in an expansive moment. Reimagine the possibilities through the lens of Me; jettison the stale, old formulas, and you will tap into a wellspring of creativity and profitability. Who knows what *Me*tail, through any iteration of the consumer industry, will look like tomorrow, next month, next year, or a decade from now? Your kids could be ordering their own customizable toys that they can receive via the family's 3D printer at home (the customization and convenience models). The standard carbon-neutral supply chain of your favorite fast-fashion retailer could take your old clothes, from any brand, to repurpose or upcycle them into new styles so that you can feel good about your carbon footprint, which is already happening at retailer Primark (the community model). As you adapt these evolving Cs to your own strengths, you will be catering to this sophisticated, powerful Me in ways that are smart, focused, and efficient, with limitless possibilities for growth.

So once and for all, stop thinking that this *Me*tail revolution is about incorporating the internet or "omnichannel" or about the Kardashians or live shopping. . . . Focusing on the latest fad tactics is missing the point; employ them, but only if they support your Cs. Again, it's the people who are in charge. The Me's. I know that can be scary for leaders, who are taught to "control the controllable." How do you control anything in a world where you are no longer calling the shots?

If I were to tell you I have all the answers, I would be either lying or delusional. This is a time of major transition, and the revolution could take on an infinite number of shapes. But what I do know is that pretty much everything you have been doing up until this point has to be rethought. The multifaceted solution lies in distilling the range of possibilities that could motivate Me's to join your cause, buy your product, or talk about your brand down to its very essence. In other words, the Cs. The rest is up to you.

ACKNOWLEDGMENTS

Some people collect baseball cards or Beanie Babies or NFTs. I collect people. My life has been richer for the hundreds of relationships that taught me thousands of lessons. I cannot possibly name everyone who matters to me, but I'd like to acknowledge a few whose patience, counsel, and challenge helped hone my personal and professional philosophy and performance ethic.

To the Godfather of Granite, Rich: Thank you for teaching me the art of selling and the value of doing a job right. I loved my years on the tile truck.

To My Bates Crew: Bobcats forever.

To Carla: Nobody taught me more about the "art" of life. Your poise, self-confidence, and take-no-prisoners attitude are just a lethal combination. I have no idea what web of embellishments you wrote to the admissions department at HBS, but it deserves a place in the letter-of-recommendation hall of fame.

To Bill: What CEO answers his phone at home on a Sunday and hands a 24-year-old a job he's totally unqualified for? You taught me how to remain positive in the face of adversity and especially the importance of managing cash in a crisis!

To my Letts of London gang (*Peaky Blinders*, we were not): I still can only understand every third word you say, but it makes me happy we have remained friends for all these years.

To Thano, my friend since eighth grade: Nobody has ever pushed me harder. Can you please lay off now?

To AJ, my twin: Your presence in my life has brought me into balance more times than you'll ever know.

To Sterno, Durks, Jimmy C, Fresh Teddy, Bigz, Welch, Tex, Mike, Hobby, Gordo, Joey D, Rubes, House, Roghay, and the rest of my b-school friends: Thank you for treating a joker like me as though he belonged and for building up my confidence in between the "short" jokes.

To Jay M.: Anyone who witnessed our first meeting would never have guessed how strong our relationship would grow. I count you as a friend, a mentor, a counselor, a life guide, and so much more. How many times did you patiently talk me off how many ledges?

To Hoff: I have never met anyone with better instincts about building a business, nor with more loyalty to his people. When I needed you to come to my (self-inflicted) defense, you showed up. I wish I hadn't needed you to show up so many times since, but you've been there, every single time, protecting me, mostly from me. Thank you.

To Fred: I was right. When you were promoted to CEO, it was the best thing that ever happened . . . to me. You gave me the tools and trusted me with your relationships, which is the greatest gift you could have offered.

To Dave B.: I'm thankful every day for our Venn diagram overlap. What a journey it has been and what a journey it will be. We make an unstoppable team.

To my clients: It's one of my life's great joys to be able to call you my friends and not just my clients. I can't name you, but you know who you are.

To Al, Holly, Lisa, Michael, Deb, Jim, and so many more of my restructuring colleagues: Thank you for teaching me the foundational lessons and for showing me what true excellence is all about.

To Lisa C.: You put the C in CFO. My sister from another mother [fist bump emoji].

To my global retail crew: Can there ever have been a more talented group, working as one team for one common goal? You are the reason I work, and you make me so proud every day.

To my OG retail crew, Schmitt, Sonia, Murali, Ash, Webb, Jimbo, Frate-Train, Meiras, Schneids: Thank you for all the times we [*censored*].

To Mark N.: Whatever "they" will pay you for the tell-all, I'll double it. Thank you for keeping my secrets and keeping me sane.

To my extended family and friends: Thank you, from the bottom of my heart, for giving me more love and support than I deserve.

To Donya: Thank you for believing in this idea and for your time and dedication in helping make it happen.

To B.G.: I know it's trite but it's also true. You are the hardest working agent in show business. You demonstrate your expertise and dedication in so many ways and it is clear you care deeply about this project but also about me and I thank you.

To Patty W.: I couldn't have hoped for a better editor. Thank you for your enthusiasm, partnership, and especially for understanding me and allowing me to work the way I like to work, even when it might have made your job more difficult.

And finally, to Samantha Marshall: Sam, you were my book whisperer and my constant companion every step of the way. There is simply no way this book would exist if not for you. I knew from our first meeting you were the one for me, and it is with the deepest gratitude that I now say thank you.

NOTES

Chapter 1

1. Feinberg, Richard A., and Meoli, Jennifer, "A Brief History of the Mall," *Advances in Consumer Research*, 1991, Vol. 18, pp. 426–442, https://www.acrwebsite.org/volumes/7196/volumes/v18/NA(-)18%7C.

2. Crawford, Fred, and Mathews, Ryan, *The Myth of Excellence: Why Great Companies Never Try to Be the Best at Everything*, New York: Currency, reprint edition, 2003, https://www.amazon.com/Myth-Excellence-Great-Companies-Everything/dp/0609810014.

3. Newton, Casey, "Facebook Pivots to Audio," *The Verge and Platformer*, April 20, 2021, https://www.theverge.com/2021/4/20/22394215/facebook-soundbites-audio-mark-zuckerberg-interview.

4. Wahba, Phil, "A Record 12,200 U.S. Stores Closed in 2020 as E-commerce, Pandemic Changed Retail Forever," *Fortune*, January 7, 2021, https://fortune.com/2021/01/07/record-store-closings-bankruptcy-2020/#:~:text=A%20record%2012%2C200%20U.S.%20stores,commerce%2C%20pandemic%20changed%20retail%20forever&text=When%20it%2comes%20to%20store,year%20for%20the%20record%20books.

5. Coppola, Daniela, "Quarterly Share of E-commerce Sales of Total U.S. Retail Sales from 1st Quarter 2010 to 1st Quarter 2021," *Statista*, May 28, 2021, https://www.statista.com/statistics/187439/share-of-e-commerce-sales-in-total-us-retail-sales-in-2010/.

6. Rupp, Lindsey, Whiteaker, Chloe, Townsend, Matt, and Bhasin, Kim, "The Death of Clothing," *Bloomberg*, February 5, 2018, https://www.bloomberg .com/graphics/2018-death-of-clothing/.

7. "Target Corporation Reports Fourth Quarter and Full-Year 2020 Earnings," *A Bull's Eye View* (Target corporate newsletter), March 2, 2021, https://investors.target.com/news-releases/news-release-details/target -corporation-reports-fourth-quarter-and-full-year-2020#:~:text=Full %2DYear%202020%20Highlights,growth%20in%20digital%20 comparable%20sales.

8. Bertoni, Steven, "Target Sales Just Shocked Wall Street—Here's How CEO Brian Cornell Did It," *Forbes*, November 18, 2020, https://www.forbes .com/sites/stevenbertoni/2020/11/18/target-sales-just-shocked-wall-street -heres-how-ceo-brian-cornell-did-it/?sh=7ab1c83e7641.

Chapter 2

1. Ebert, Roger, "Plowing Fields Won't Grow Business," *Roger Ebert.com*, September 22, 2005, https://www.rogerebert.com/roger-ebert/plowing -fields-wont-grow-business.

Chapter 3

1. Danziger, Pamela N., "5 Reasons That Glossier Is So Successful," *Forbes*, November 7, 2018, https://www.forbes.com/sites/pamdanziger/ 2018/11/07/5-keys-to-beauty-brand-glossiers-success/?sh=6e08fb82417d.

Chapter 4

1. Kindy, David, "Cleaner Version of Building #19 Opens Next Week in Plymouth," *Patriot Ledger*, October 25, 2019, https://www.patriotledger .com/news/20191025/cleaner-version-of-building-19-opens-next-week -in-plymouth.

2. Miranda, Leticia, "Thousands of Retail Stores Are Closing—So How Is Dollar General Opening Almost 20 Stores a Week?" NBCNews.com, December 5, 2019, https://www.nbcnews.com/business/consumer/thou- sands-retail-stores-are-closing-so-how-dollar-general-opening-n1095791.

3. Telford, Taylor, "Five Below Is a Wonderland of Things No One Needs. It's Also One of the Most Successful Retailers in America," *Washington Post*, December 28, 2018, https://www.washingtonpost.com/business/ 2018/12/28/five-below-is-wonderland-things-no-one-needs-its-also-one -most-successful-retailers-america/.

4. Chen, Connie, "Italic Is a Membership-Based Retailer That Sells Luxury Bags, Clothing, and Home Goods Made in the Same Factories as Brands like Prada, Alo Yoga, and All-Clad—Here's How Its Products Stack Up, and Why We Think the Membership Fee Is Worth It," *BusinessInsider.com*,

October 5, 2020, https://www.businessinsider.com/italic-review-luxury -brandless-bags.

5. Channick, Robert, "Cricket Wireless President Expanding Beyond Chicago Base," *Chicago Tribune*, December 29, 2016 https://www.chicagotribune.com/ business/ct-cricket-wireless-dwyer-exec-qa-0101-biz-20161228-story.html.

6. Sanspotter, Scott, "EasyJet Vs. Ryanair: The Battle to Be the Stingiest Airline on Planet Earth," *Sanspotter.com* (n.d.), https://www.sanspotter.com/easyjet -vs-ryanair/.

7. Anderson, George, "What Walmart Learned from Its 'Fast Fail' with Jetblack," *Forbes*, February 19, 2020, https://www.forbes.com/sites/retailwire/2020/02/ 19/what-walmart-learned-from-its-fast-fail-with-jet-black/?sh=69324ba23cd4.

Chapter 5

1. Boulton, Clint, "Wawa Brings Digital Integration to the Convenience Store," *CIO*, April 29, 2019, https://www.cio.com/article/3391396/wawa-brings -digital-integration-to-the-convenience-store.html.

2. McCarthy, Amy, "How Buc-ee's Became Texas's Most Beloved Road Trip Destination," *Eater,* June 14, 2017, https://www.eater.com/2017/6/14/ 15795244/buc-ees-texas-most-beloved-road-trip-destination.

3. Seiders, Kathleen, Berry, Leonard L., and Gresham, Larry G., "Attention, Retailers! How Convenient Is Your Convenience Strategy?" *MIT Sloan Management Review*, April 15, 2000, https://sloanreview.mit.edu/article/ attention-retailers-how-convenient-is-your-convenience-strategy/.

4. Kapner, Suzanne, "Stores Have a Mission: Getting You to Keep That Thing You Bought Online," *Wall Street Journal*, February 9, 2021, https://www .wsj.com/articles/stores-have-a-mission-getting-you-to-keep-that-thing -you-bought-online-11612866602.

5. Fine, Jenny B., "Target and Ulta Beauty Team Up," *Women's Wear Daily*, November 10, 2020, https://wwd.com/beauty-industry-nws/beauty-features/ target-ulta-beauty-partnership-team-up-1234654480/.

Chapter 6

1. Stewart, James B., "Underdog Against Amazon, Best Buy Charges Ahead," *New York Times,* December 13, 2013, https://www.nytimes.com/2013/ 12/14/business/fast-rise-of-best-buy-in-the-face-of-amazon.html.

2. Howland, Daphne, "And the Winner of the Latest Amazon–Best Buy Deal Is . . . ," *Retail Dive,* April 18, 2018, https://www.retaildive.com/news/and -the-winner-of-the-latest-amazon-best-buy-deal-is/521694/.

3. Merwin, Hugh, "The Absolute Best Wine Shops in New York," *Grub Street* (blog), April 25, 2018, https://www.grubstreet.com/bestofnewyork/absolute -best-wine-shops-nyc.html.

4. Sonsev, Veronika, "Sephora Shows How Inclusivity Is Good for Business," *Forbes*, February 10, 2021, https://www.forbes.com/sites/veronikasonsev/2021/02/10/sephora-shows-how-inclusivity-is-good-for-business/?sh=59afb68fc48f/.

Chapter 7

1. Ernest, Maya, "Nike Will Soon Let You Design Your Own Dunk Low Sneaker," *Input Magazine,* January 4, 2021, https://www.inputmag.com/style/nike-dunk-low-nike-by-you-sneaker-customization.
2. Bain, Marc, "A Pair of Rare Nike Sneakers May Be the Key to Catching a Washington Riot Suspect," *Quartz*, January 12, 2021, https://qz.com/1956057/nike-shoes-may-be-the-key-to-catching-washington-riot-suspect/.
3. Stieghorst, Tom, "Getting Personal," *Travel Weekly*, April 3, 2019, https://www.travelweekly.com/Cruise-Travel/Focus-on-Cruise-Getting-personal.

Chapter 8

1. Jansen, Caroline, "A Closer Look at RH's Aspen 'Ecosystem,'" *Retail Dive*, January 14, 2021, https://www.retaildive.com/news/a-closer-look-at-rhs-aspen-ecosystem/593272/.
2. Stone, Madeline, "We Flew to the Hamptons Like the 1% with Blade, an 'Uber-for-Helicopters' Startup—and It Was as Fabulous as It Sounds," *Business Insider*, September 11, 2015, https://sg.finance.yahoo.com/news/flew-hamptons-1-blade-uber-154556280.html.

Chapter 9

1. Sherman, Lauren, "How to Build a Customer-Centric Brand," *Business of Fashion,* October 30, 2020, https://www.businessoffashion.com/case-studies/retail/case-study-fashion-brand-management-urban-outfitters-anthropologie-free-people.
2. Sherman, Lauren, "Will Anthropologie Win Where Traditional Department Stores Have Failed?" *Business of Fashion,* October 11, 2016, https://www.businessoffashion.com/articles/retail/anthropologie-super-store.
3. "Fashion on Climate," http://www2.globalfashionagenda.com/initiatives/fashion-on-climate/#/our-impact.
4. "Fashion Industry Waste Statistics," *EDGE*, https://edgexpo.com/fashion-industry-waste-statistics/.
5. Ponce de Leon, Sandra, "How thredUP Is Driving the Circular Fashion Movement . . ." *Forbes*, August 27, 2019, https://www.forbes.com/sites/cognitiveworld/2019/08/27/how-thredup-circular-fashion-ai/?sh=3a09137879a0.

INDEX

ABOUT
THE AUTHOR

Veteran change agent **Joel Bines** has brought his trademark hands-on approach to a diverse array of businesses for almost 30 years. He is one of the world's leading operational strategists, having helped navigate change at dozens of companies.

Joel's conversation with consumers began with summer jobs in high school and continues to this day. Always a "lunch-pail-and-hard-hat" kind of guy, Joel has a work ethic that can be summed up with two words: "outwork everyone." After graduating from Bates College in Lewiston, Maine, with a degree in philosophy, he talked his way into a series of jobs with distressed companies facing deep challenges. His early success turning around companies led him to Harvard Business School, where he earned an MBA with Distinction in 1999. A chance meeting with legendary turnaround expert Jay Alix led him to join AlixPartners where he has spent nearly two decades.

Joel is a member of the board of directors of the Martin Luther King Jr. Memorial Foundation and a trustee of TITAS/Dance Unbound.